Isolation and Paradox

Recent Titles in
Contributions in Political Science

Trotskyism and the Dilemma of Socialism
Christopher Z. Hobson and Ronald D. Tabor

Policy Studies: Integration and Evaluation
Stuart S. Nagel

Open Borders? Closed Societies? The Ethical and Political Issues
Mark Gibney, editor

Dependence, Development, and State Repression
George A. Lopez and Michael Stohl, editors

Urban Minority Administrators: Politics, Policy, and Style
Albert K. Karnig and Paula D. McClain, editors

Papers for the Millions: The New Journalism in Britain, 1850s to 1914
Joel H. Wiener, editor

Government Response to Financial Constraints
L. R. Jones and Jerry L. McCaffery

Dilemmas of Social Democracy: The Spanish Socialist Workers Party in the
1980s
Donald Share

A Staff for the President: The Executive Office, 1921–1952
Alfred Dick Sander

Hungary and the USSR, 1956–1988: Kadar's Political Leadership
Andrew Felkay

Trotsky and Djilas: Critics of Communist Bureaucracy
Michael M. Lustig

ISOLATION AND PARADOX

Defining "The Public" in Modern Political Analysis

FRANK LOUIS RUSCIANO

HM
261
.R78
1989
West

CONTRIBUTIONS IN POLITICAL SCIENCE, NUMBER 233

Bernard K. Johnpoll, Series Editor

GREENWOOD PRESS

New York • Westport, Connecticut • London

Copyright Acknowledgments

The author and publisher wish to thank the following for
permission to use copyrighted materials:

Brian Barry, *Political Argument*, Copyright © 1965 by Brian Barry. Reprinted by
permission of Routledge and Kegan Paul.

Brian Barry and Russell Hardin, *Rational Man and Irrational
Society?*, copyright © 1982 by Brian Barry and Russell Hardin.
Reprinted by permission of Sage Publications, Inc.

Russell Hardin, *Collective Action*, copyright © 1971. Published
for Resources for the Future by the Johns Hopkins University
Press.

Fred Hirsch, *The Social Limits to Growth*, copyright © 1976.
Reprinted by permission of the Harvard University Press.

Elisabeth Noelle-Neumann, *The Spiral of Silence*, copyright ©
1984 by The University of Chicago Press. Reprinted by permission
of the University of Chicago Press.

Library of Congress Cataloging-in-Publication Data

Rusciano, Frank Louis, 1954–
  Isolation and paradox.

  (Contributions in political science, ISSN
0147–1066 ; no. 233)
  Bibliography: p.
  Includes index.
  1. Public opinion.   2. Social choice.
I. Title.   II. series.
HN261.R78   1989   303.3'8   88–29626
ISBN 0–313–26492–9 (lib. bdg. : alk. paper)

British Library Cataloguing in Publication Data is available.

Copyright © 1989 by Frank Louis Rusciano

Library of Congress Catalog Card Number: 88–29626
ISBN: 0–313–26492–9
ISSN: 0147–1066

First published in 1989

Greenwood Press, Inc.
88 Post Road West, Westport, Connecticut   06881

Printed in the United States of America

The paper used in this book complies with the
Permanent Paper Standard issued by the National
Information Standards Organization (Z39.48–1984).

10 9 8 7 6 5 4 3 2 1

For Robin

Contents

Figures and Tables

FIGURES

TABLES

Foreword

This book grew out of a series of lectures and two seminars I presented as a visiting professor at the Institut für Publizistik at the University of Mainz in the German Federal Republic. I went to Mainz as an Alexander von Humboldt Fellow, planning to write a book comparing Elisabeth Noelle-Neumann's "spiral of silence" theory with classical interpretations of "public opinion." I soon discovered, however, that her ideas concerning behavioral patterns of speech and silencing had enormous implications for public choice and collective decision making. The implications led me to a major theme in classical and modern social analysis—the distinction between public and private realms in liberal societies. This theme became the controlling idea for my study.

I offer the reader several thoughts in the pages that follow. First, I assert that the supposed "paradoxes" of collective decision making under responsive rules are a price paid for accepting an inadequate notion of "public" in "public opinion" and "public choice." Noelle-Neumann's theory proposes an alternative notion of public, which I operationalize to attack three of these problems. Second, I wish to cross certain boundaries traditionally erected in social analysis, most notably those between Marxist and social-choice approaches, and behavioral and institutional approaches. I attempt to integrate these approaches wherever possible and provide new insights into their basic differences where necessary. Finally, I endeavor to fit into a laudable recent trend in public choice analysis—the notion that this topic is too important and too rich to be discussed in a manner that limits its audience to specialists and economists. I aim here at the general reader in political science who might have an interest in the common themes upon which public opinion and public choice rest.

Of course, there are risks in attempting to integrate fields in any discipline, since the lines of communication among practitioners are often not well established. On the practical side, one risks alienating persons interested in one field by speaking too much about another. I can only hope that the general themes linking these fields are compelling enough to help readers surpass this block. On the academic side, I am reminded of a comment made by a colleague after I had completed a lecture at the Allensbach Institut: "Why would you wish to develop a theory integrating fields, when you can easily end up disturbing practitioners in all of them?" I decided to interpret this question as an indication that I was on the right track, for while it is certainly not the case that all disturbing ideas are enlightening, it is inarguable that all enlightening ideas are, at least initially, somewhat disturbing. Hopefully, any disturbance caused by this work will be of the latter variety.

As with any academic work, this book would not have been possible without the support of several institutions and individuals. I am especially grateful to the Alexander von Humboldt Foundation, which provided the primary financial support for this endeavor, and which graciously extended the grant when I required more time to work on the project. The Institut für Publizistik at the University of Mainz and the Institut für Demoskopie Allensbach were also quite gracious, providing me with research assistance, access to data, and even housing for myself and my family while we were in the German Federal Republic. Finally, Rider College paid for my travel expenses when I returned to lecture and to continue my research in the Federal Republic during the summer of 1987.

An extensive list of individuals contributed support and encouragement to this book. At the University of Mainz, Dr. Wolfgang Donsbach and Professor Hans Mathias Kepplinger provided useful commentary during my lectures; my student assistants, Anna Jaeckel and Doris Kolesch, were also quite helpful. At the Institut für Demoskopie Allensbach, the statistical and support staff provided me with great amounts of useful data, often responding to rushed requests with remarkable speed and care. Dr. Kenneth Prewitt, vice president for programs at the Rockefeller Foundation, and Professor Brian Barry, presently of the London School of Economics, wrote recommendations for my initial application for the von Humboldt grant.

At Rider College, I am grateful to Dean Dominick Iorio who also wrote a recommendation for my grant application, and to the faculty travel fund for underwriting my travel to the Federal Republic to give lectures in 1987. The Political Science Department graciously recommended my leave of absence, which was approved by the College. I am also grateful to Celeste Thatcher and Wanda Guarino, who patiently typed the manuscript, and who greeted each change and correction with good humor.

Special thanks go to Dr. Jonathan Mendilow, my colleague in political science at Rider, and to Daniel Oberst, Director of Advanced Technology and Applications at Princeton University. Jonathan provided useful commentary on subsequent drafts of the book; he proved to be a sharp enough critic to catch any lapses in argument and a good enough friend to point them out to me. Dan worked magic with the book's graphics in Figures 1 to 13, starting from the crude line drawings I had provided him.

As a final note, this book owes much of its existence to two scholars with whom I have the pleasure of association. The first is Professor Elisabeth Noelle-Neumann, who invited me to the Federal Republic and who nominated me for the von Humboldt Fellowship. Without her support, there simply would have been no book. Her insight and encouragement during our conversations were a source of inspiration while I was writing this work. The second person is my wife Robin, who encouraged me, tolerating the alternating moods of elation and despair which accompany such a project. More important, however, were the critical insights she provided concerning silencing processes from her own work in the Federal Republic. This book is much richer for our countless conversations on this subject.

1

The Dilemma

It is one of the peculiar ironies in modern social analysis that we have abandoned our sense of the notion "public." This circumstance is peculiar because a major concern in political thought is the definition of the public realm and the rights and duties of the public person. It is ironic because we still make wide use of the term public in a manner that often belies its original purposes. The term pervades descriptions of topics in several social science disciplines, particularly political science—public policy, public administration, public health, public law, public opinion, and public choice, to name but a few examples. In these cases, "public" commonly serves as a prefix meaning "regarding or related to the state." "The public" and the "public realm" thus depend upon the existence and actions of the state for definition.

The problems of associating "the public" with the actions of the state are perhaps most acute for the concepts of public opinion and public choice. Both concepts are damaged by a dependence upon government for definition, since both were originally assumed, in liberal theory, to have a very different relationship to the state. By losing track of the actual sense of "public" in both concepts, we generate contradictions in our analysis of political decision making and institutions. By recovering the sense of public in "public choice" through a new understanding of public in "public opinion," we ease many of these contradictions.

What follows proceeds in two steps. First, I illustrate how the modern interpretation of "public" affects the notion of "public opinion." Second, I discuss how this effect carries over into the analysis of public choice, making that area of inquiry incapable of defining its own subject matter. Certain so-called paradoxes of public choice are symptomatic of this problem. This procedure introduces the problem that will be addressed in the second chapter. There, I propose an alternative definition of "public," operationalized from a new theory of public opinion, to deal with these paradoxes.

THE "PUBLIC" IN PUBLIC OPINION

It has become unpopular in modern social analyses to speak of "the public." The concept is considered a holdover from a more naive time in social analysis, a notion too vague to be useful, even while it is a necessary assumption for positive political theory. We accept David Hume's admonition that "All governments rest on opinion" in liberal theory (Hume, 1963:29) but treat this insight as an embarrassing aside. Indeed, "the public" in liberal thought has become much like the God of certain modern theologians—a "first mover" who appears at the moment of creation and then disappears from the realm of human activity. "The public" was present at the moment of the state's inception and expressed a "public opinion" in a covenant that legitimized the state in a precivil society condition. Such expression was the public's last creative act, for thereafter, it ceased to have an existence separate from the state it created. The determination of public and private realms was turned over to the government, despite attempts to determine public and private dimensions independently of the state. In *On Liberty*, for instance, Mill attempts to deal with the distinction between "self-regarding" and "other-regarding" issues in society (Mill 1956:91–113), but concludes in an unsatisfactory manner. His failure underscores the difficulty of attempting to define the public realm by beginning with individual preferences, a subject to which I will return in due course.[1]

"The public" thus serves as a first assumption of questionable existence, somewhere between hypothetical construct and myth. This sense of public does irreparable harm to the notion of "public opinion." Consider one of the most widely accepted definitions of public opinion, from V. O. Key's classic study: "those opinions held by private persons which government finds it prudent to heed" (Key, 1961:14).[2] Opinion, so defined, derives its public quality not from its association with a "public," but from its association with the state, for without a state to "heed" particular opinions, public opinion would not exist. Hume's insight is lost in tautology here. For if government is to rest upon public opinion, public opinion must precede the existence of the state; but if public opinion is defined by the government, the state must precede the existence of public opinion.

A possible response to this complaint could be that it is based upon a hypothetical construct (the "public" in the precivil society condition) whose existence no one truly accepts. But the problem, abstract as it may seem, has clear practical ramifications. Consider an example from public law. In the case of *Miller v. California* (1973), the Supreme Court of the United States was charged with considering the constitutionality of laws regarding obscenity. The judges decided that while obscene materials were not protected by the First Amendment, the judgment of what was obscene could not be rendered on the national level. Obscenity would be judged according to the values and mores of the "average person" in localities where the materials were disseminated (Mason, et al., 1983:552). The judgment of the "average person" would be determined by the application of "contemporary community standards" (Mason, et al., 1983:554). The Court's decision was based upon a common sense interpretation of national practices:

It is neither realistic nor constitutionally sound to read the First Amendment as requiring that the people of Maine or Mississippi accept *public* depiction of conduct found tolerable in Las Vegas, or New York City. People in different states *vary in their tastes and attitudes*, and this diversity is not to be strangled by the absolutism of imposed uniformity. (Mason, et al., 1983; emphases mine)

The common sense reasoning behind this decision reveals the impossibility of setting public standards for obscenity at any level guided by the opinions of the "public," rather than the decisions of the state. The court's position was that the national state shall not determine what is obscene, as that decision will be left up to state and local governments; there are no "national standards" for what is obscene; and what standards exist refer to community norms or values regarding the public display of materials. In effect, standards are set by the public opinion of the communities or states in which regulations are decided. This, however, raises the question of definition. The state opts out of deciding what is obscene because it cannot turn this decision over to a national "public" that does not exist. Hence, no national standards exist. The justices then fall back on a strategy used by many analysts of public opinion—there may be no "public," but there are a plurality of "publics" to define values, norms, or attitudes, based upon location (or class, ethnicity, sex, or a host of other factors, see Key, 1961:10). "Community standards" thus become the "opinions of publics" defined by location.

But why should such local "publics" have any more legitimate existence than the national "public" that does not exist? After all, pluralizing the notion of "public" does not define it. What percentage of persons in a community, state, or nation for that matter, must define a material obscene before the community (i.e., *public*) standard is set? If such a standard may be set by some arbitrary percentage of persons on the local or state level, why may it not be similarly defined on the national level? If a "public" may not be defined nationally, it may not be defined on a lower level of analysis either. At all levels of state decision making, the legitimacy of public decisions—if "public" should not be properly defined by the state—become questionable without a prior sense of "public" in public opinion.[3]

THE "PUBLIC" IN PUBLIC CHOICE

This problem, and others like it, provided the impetus for the field of public choice. The mandate for this field of inquiry was spelled out clearly in a definition by Kenneth Arrow: "Narrowly construed, the scope of [social choice theory] is the analysis of conditions under which some mechanism may be found which permits a collectivity (government, social organization, labor union, business) to arrive at decisions which, in one way or another, reflect the decisions desired by their members" (Arrow, 1982:252). By stepping back from the state and beginning with individual preferences, public choice theorists attempted to wrest sovereignty over public decisions back from the state (or any authoritative body) and return it to constituent individual preferences. They were guided in this endeavor by economic theorists who began with individual behavior to model the movements of the market, for if the consumer drove market decisions, there should be some means by which the citizen could drive state decisions.

The difficulty with this mandate is that public choice theory encounters problems carried over from the inadequate definition of "public" in public opinion. For public opinion precedes public choice. It is for this reason that there are natural linkages between the two fields. Consider that opinions (or preferences) are the stuff from which responsive social choices are constructed. The path from opinions to choices may be complex but it is a necessary path. Indeed, the early vogue in public choice analysis, before it became primarily a theoretical field, involved testing choice models using public opinion data.[4] By contrast, it is appropriate to discuss public administration or public health, for example, without extensive reference to opinions in most cases.

A less direct, but important, link between the two fields exists because public choice analysis is based upon economic models and consumer behavior. Consumer and market research, in turn, is a branch of public opinion research. Analysts who study the measurement and change of preferences in the market should have relevant insights for those who study the aggregation of these preferences in market and social behavior.

The theoretical discussion of the relationship between public opinion and public choice has tended to be neglected, however. The indexes of several classic works in public choice contain little more than a passing reference, if that, to public opinion. This may be due, at least in part, to a common perception that public opinion research tends to be low in theoretical content—a perception supported by the fact that social scientists have generally tended to define public opinion to serve the purposes of their research (Yeric and Todd, 1983:2). Harwood Childs, for example, was able to collect over fifty definitions of the term "public opinion" from various authors in the mid–1960s (Childs, 1965:14–26). Consequently, it is not surprising that public opinion research has tended to be viewed by social choice theorists more as a source of usable data than usable concepts.

Public choice analysis cannot escape considerations of public opinion, for the theoretical deficiencies of public opinion analysis appear in certain classic paradoxes of public choice. Both fields suffer from an underdeveloped notion of public in their accepted definitions. The paradoxes of public choice are symptomatic of this problem, which becomes evident when one attempts to define the public realm by using any responsive choice procedure. To illustrate this point, let us begin with Barry's summary of the most commonly accepted definitions of "public" in public choice, as stated by George Lewis:

A hundred and fifty years ago, Sir George Cornwall Lewis offered a general definition of "public" which it is impossible to improve upon:

Public as opposed to *private*, is that which has no immediate relation to any specific person or persons but may directly concern any member or members of the community, without distinction. Thus, the acts of a magistrate, or a member of a legislative assembly, done by them in those capacities, are called public; the acts done by the same persons towards their family or friends, or in their dealings with strangers for their own peculiar purposes, are called private. So a theatre, a place of amusement, is said to be public, not because it is actually visited by every member of the community, but because it is open to all indifferently, and any person may, if he desires, enter it. The same remark applies to public houses, public rooms, public meetings, etc. The publication of a book is the exposing of it to sale in such a manner that it may be procured by any person who desires to purchase it: it would be legally published, if not a single copy were sold. In the language of our law, public appears to be distinguished from private acts of parliament, on the ground that one class directly affects the community, the other some person or persons. (Barry, 65:190–91)

This definition has three distinct parts. First, "public" deals with issues that concern the general welfare ("that which may concern any member or members of a community," or those acts which "directly affect the community"). Second, "public" implies the impossibility of exclusion (for example, public places are those that are "open to all indifferently"). Finally, "public" implies the existence of a governmental or authoritative body to make decisions ("the acts of Magistrates . . . done by them in those capacities"). All three parts of this definition figure in Arrow's description of "public choice." We assume that when members contribute their opinions to a decision, the combination of those opinions (by whatever procedure) defines the general welfare. Arrow explicitly endorses this notion of "general welfare" in his notion of a "social welfare function" (Arrow, 1963:25). Second, we assume that group decisions are binding upon all, so that no members may be excluded from the decisions' effects (whether those effects by privileges of access or costs). Finally, we assume that any authoritative body's decisions are reached by procedures that are generally recognized as legitimate by group members.

None of these definitions however, capture the notion of "public" in "public choice." To illustrate this point, let us consider the derivation of each notion of public described above using any social choice procedure and judge what is missing in all three cases, by asking three questions. First, how are issues that constitute the "general welfare" decided, for example those issues with which social choices are to be concerned? Second, how are goods described by the "impossibility of exclusion" defined or created? Third, from where does the legitimacy of a decision-making procedure or an authoritative body arise? In other words, how are public issues distinguished from private issues, public goods from private goods, and legitimate public decision processes from illegitimate processes, respectively. The obvious answer to these questions, in keeping with the spirit of social choice, is that these decisions are made by applying some responsive choice procedure to the alternatives. The problem with this answer (ignoring the possible infinite regress of trying to select choice procedures to make choices) is that it is impossible to respond to these questions consistently, assuming a minimal degree of disagreement among self-interested voters. Without a prior definition of "public" in "public choice" to direct us toward the proper topics for choice procedures, the field of public choice must, in practice, define its own boundaries. The supposed "paradoxes" of public choice are symptomatic of the general impossibility of this task.

Regarding issues that concern or constitute the "general welfare," Arrow has shown that it is impossible to define a responsive social welfare function meeting minimal conditions, without dictatorial intervention in many cases (Arrow, 1963). Arrow's description of the ranking of "social states" may also be applied to the selection of issues that form the agenda for social decisions. Let us attempt to distinguish those issues that fall into the public realm (and are thus suitable subjects for public choice) from those issues that should remain in the private realm. Assume that with no action, the issue remains private; three choices may be defined in setting an agenda using two issues, A and B. First, A may be a public issue and B may be left private; call this choice x. Second,

B may be a public issue and *A* may be left private; call this choice *y*. Third, both *A* and *B* may be public issues; call this choice *z*. The Voter's Paradox or the problem of cyclical group preferences may be encountered if any responsive decision procedure is used to choose between these alternatives for a public agenda. Using the classic example, consider the result if majority rule is applied to the ranking of pairs of alternatives in a three person group with the following preferences:

	Person 1	Person 2	Person 3
first choice:	x	y	z
second choice:	y	z	x
third choice:	z	x	y

If the alternative pairs are considered in the following order—(*x*, *y*), (*y*, *z*), (*z*, *x*)—*x* is preferred to *y*, *y* is preferred to *z*, and *z* is preferred to *x*. Furthermore, assume that *w* is the fourth, or last choice of all three voters; *w* represents the case where neither issue appears on the public agenda. Without a decision, both issues remain in the private realm. W is the outcome, which no voter prefers. Considering the issues as dichotomous choices will not help; we would still arrive at one of four outcomes: *x*, *y*, *z*, or *w*. Yet, each of these outcomes can be defeated by at least one of the other outcomes in majority voting.

These conclusions will hold for any decision rule based upon the preferences of individual members. With reference to the "general welfare," no public choice procedure may consistently define its own subject matter. The "sting" in this problem is that it is virtually assured to appear in any society with a wide variety of potential public issues and minimal disagreement over classifying them.[5]

What of the definition of goods described by the impossibility of exclusion, using some form of public choice procedure? Here, "public goods" must be distinguished from "private goods," and we encounter the problem described by Olson (1965)—that is, the creation of public goods by rationally minded individuals may be impossible. Consider the example of public television. All may desire public television, and be willing to contribute to its establishment and maintenance if the only alternative was that it would not otherwise exist, but there is another set of alternatives. Each individual who desires this service would find it optimal to enjoy this benefit without having to contribute to its cost, by allowing others to pay for it. All persons may also believe that their contribution is inconsequential, since it is unlikely to make the difference between public television's existence or demise. If all persons behave in this manner, the collective good will only be provided under very restrictive circumstances. These circumstances are when one person feels it is in his interest to pay the entire cost of the collective good, when selective incentives are offered to individuals who contribute, or when individuals are somehow coerced to contribute, usually by some authoritative body (see Olson, 1965, chapter 6). All goods will tend to remain private goods, despite the opinions of the individual members that this is a nonoptimal solution. If public goods cannot be created, however, public and private goods may not be distinguished by any decision process. If public choice deals with such goods, it deals with an empty set; once again, no choice procedure may consistently describe the field's subject matter.

It is useful to review Olson's solution to this problem. The first solution, where one individual pays the entire cost of the collective good, merely restates the above point; the collective good exists because it is reinterpreted as a private good by the individual providing it. The second two solutions—selective incentives for contributors or penalties for non-contributors—require some authoritative body to link impossibility of exclusion from the benefits of a collective good to impossibility of exclusion from contributing to its costs. This solution falls into the realm of the third notion of "public" endorsed by public choice theorists; unfortunately, a version of the Olson problem also occurs here. It may be in my interests to accept the "collective good" of majority rule with minimal enforcement costs (to use democracy as an example of a system governed by responsive rules); yet, I may not wish to "pay" the cost of obedience when it conflicts with my interests to pay.

This problem merits special attention outside of Olson's framework. At issue here are the conditions under which "legitimate" rules may be established for public choice decisions. Legitimate rules are rules generally perceived as just and worthy of obedience by the persons they govern. Legitimacy thus implies a third public/private distinction for group members: under what conditions do we surrender decisions, and the power to coerce, to public procedures, instead of relying upon our own private decisions to direct our actions? This question raises some peculiar problems, for as Arrow notes, the choice of a decision procedure is in itself the result of a decision procedure (Arrow, 1963:89–91). But it is impossible to use a decision process to prove its own validity (and legitimacy), since any system of rules or axioms for decision making or evaluation must contain rules that are unprovable within the system. Conditions may be set so that we are reasonably sure a decision procedure is generally regarded as legitimate, however. Barry considers this question for the specific case of majority rule in "Is Democracy Special?" He discovers that majority choice may legitimize democracy (or rule by majority), but only under fairly restrictive conditions (Barry, 1979:172–85). Let us deal with the derivative of conditions for a more general case of this problem, involving any decision rule considered as a means of making authoritative group choices.

I wish to prove that any decision process that provides justification for its own use must, as a necessary condition, eliminate all other possible processes. Let us consider a decision process and refer to it as Procedure X. We would only be justified in using Procedure X to evaluate decision systems if we believed this procedure to be the best for deciding among alternatives in a given set. Consider the simplest case where only two decision systems are to be considered for governing a group: Procedure X, and another arrangement, Procedure Y.

Is Procedure Y a viable alternative? If it is, then it must have some possibility of being chosen to make group choices. If it is not a viable alternative, then Procedure X must be a *privileged choice* as an outcome, since the alternative has been eliminated. Procedure Y would be an irrational choice as a decision system because Procedure X was defined as the best means of evaluating alternatives. However, if Procedure X is used to evaluate decision rules, and Procedure X is not a privileged choice in this process, then Procedure Y may be chosen (according to the above definition of a privileged choice).

Because Procedure Y may not be chosen, then, either Procedure X may not be used to evaluate alternatives, or Procedure X must be a privileged choice whenever it is used to select a decision process. The first possibility is rejected on practical and logical grounds. Practically, Procedure X is assumed to be the best means of making a decision, yet the first supposition states that this procedure may not be used. But it would be an irrational choice to decide according to an inferior procedure (if we decide at all). Logically, the first supposition implies the absurd conclusion that if Procedure X is used to evaluate choices, then Procedure X may not be used to evaluate choices. Hence, a minimal condition for a procedure's axiomatic status is that it eliminate all other alternative procedures for making choices. This result will be referred to later in the text as the *Rule of Privileged Choice*. It may be restated in a simple, intuitively satisfying manner: if Procedure X is used to select a decision process other than Procedure X, then we should not have used Procedure X to make this decision in the first place.[6]

However, how restrictive is this condition? It does not prove that Procedure X is the best process for evaluating alternatives, rather, when violated, the condition disproves this assumption.[7] This condition provides a rough-and-ready means of empirically testing whether evaluative results support the use of an axiomatic principle (or combination of principles). If a principle (or principles) does not eliminate all other decision rules, it cannot be assumed the best decision procedure. If that principle does eliminate all other decision rules, then its acceptability as an axiomatic principle is supported—but not proved—in the instance being considered. If the axiomatic principle contains only one rule, this rule is a privileged rule. If the axiom (or decision procedure) contains two or more separate rules, the matter is a more complex possibility I will consider in chapter 3.

Given the Rule of Privileged Choice, may any rules based upon the preferences of group members fulfill this condition, to be granted axiomatic status as legitimate privileged rules? The answer is "yes," but only in a manner that further damages the accepted notions of "public" in public choice. Unanimous decision making is the only rule that always eliminates all other possible decision rules, since it defines the entire group as the smallest decisive subset for reaching a decision. Any rule that is less than unanimous risks being declared illegitimate by members of the potential minority (regardless of how small that minority is).

But if a potential minority may declare a less than unanimous rule illegitimate for reaching decisions, then that rule should not have been used in the first place to evaluate alternative decision procedures. It thus may not be an axiomatic principle. The members of any minority on a decision may always declare the original procedure by which decision rules were evaluated to be invalid, if they object to the outcomes of any particular decision reached under that procedure. Or, if any members anticipate being in the minority while a decision procedure is being chosen, they will veto all procedures short of unanimous rule. Any minority on any decision may thus delegitimize the system.

How serious a problem is this for advocates of responsive choice procedures? First, it is likely that in the original choice of decision procedures, "People voting on political and economic arrangements are not simply choosing a set of rules on the understanding they will have an equal chance of getting assigned any role; they have a fairly distinct idea of the general position they will occupy" (Barry, 1965:200). Of course, people who expect to be members of the decision majority could simply coerce the minority to accept their decision rules; but then we have strayed far from public choice assumptions in relying upon coercion to legitimize decision rules.

The quandary is, however, that we also stray from public choice assumptions when we reject this argument in favor of unanimous rule. Recall the question with which we began: when will the individual surrender his private decisions to a group decision process, thereby rendering that process legitimate? With unanimous rule, the answer is "never." Since no group decision may be reached unless the public decision corresponds to every person's private decision, the individual surrenders no power to the decision making process. All public decisions collapse into private decisions, and "public choice" once again becomes a field devoid of substantive content.

Let us now take stock of where we are. I have shown that no public choice procedure may distinguish consistently between public and private issues, public and private goods, and public and private decision rules. As such, no procedure may consistently define the "public" realm implied by the term's definition. The "paradoxes" of public choice—notably Arrow's General Possibility theorem, Olson's logic of collective action, and Barry's problem of legitimizing responsive choice procedures—are illustrations of this problem. A group must have a prior consensus concerning the content of the general welfare, the definition of public goods, and the legitimacy of decision processes before public choice has a defined realm in which to practice. But when we speak of prior consensus, we are discussing the conditions of public opinion that must exist prior to public choice in a society or group.

It is here that social choice theorists could understandably cry foul, accusing us of falling victim to our own arguments. For how is public opinion constructed, if not out of individual opinions? And if we must combine individual opinions (by whatever additive procedure), we are at the same stumbling block mentioned above; that is, how may one aggregate individual preferences into "public opinion" without running into the now familiar problems of defining the public realm? This question would be reasonable (and indeed, unanswerable) if we remained within the traditional definitions of "public."

In the following chapter, I go beyond the prior definitions of "public," in favor of a new definition advanced by Elisabeth Noelle-Neumann in her "spiral of silence" theory. The second chapter derives from her theory three propositions, or theorems, that describe the transformation of individual opinions into public opinion, from which public choices may be made. These theorems are applied to the "paradoxes" of public choice in chapter 4.

Chapter 3 is a brief, but necessary, elaboration of the discussions in chapter 2 concerning the notion of "public" and the Arrow problem, the logic of collective action, and the difficulty of legitimizing responsive decision systems. Here, the axiomatic underpinnings of Arrow's proof are abstracted in terms of a general typology of decision rules. This process accomplishes two things. First, it allows the Arrow problem to be addressed on the most general level by the derived propositions. Second, it proves that the logic of collective action and the problem of responsive legitimacy are actually versions of the Arrow problem.

Chapter 4 applies the alternative notion of public, operationalized in the derived theorems, to the three paradoxes. This application has two purposes: to prove that the theorems describe a reasonable solution to the problem and to show this solution to be the most acceptable for advocates of responsive decision systems. Past solutions to the problem, including Marx's response, are examined briefly to illustrate this point.

Chapter 5 begins with a theoretical application of the previous chapter's argument, first to economic behavior through a critique of Fred Hirsch's *Social Limits to Growth*, and then to the problem of collective action. The chapter concludes with a formal model and three hypotheses that are tested in chapters 6 and 7. In chapter 6, the hypotheses are tested through empirical analyses of classic problems in collective action and choice. In chapter 7, these hypotheses are tested as models of a revised notion of "social preference" suggested by the theorems from chapter 2. The revised notion is illustrated by observations about consumer behavior, conventions of language, and the definition and functions of social and state institutions. This new idea of "social preference" is then traced back to the revised notion of "public" Noelle-Neumann introduces in her theory.

As a final note on method, this book is not intended as a comprehensive review of public opinion or public choice literature. My purpose is to consider how the common ground defined by both subjects' use of the notion "public" can direct us to revitalizing the term in modern social analysis. For the loss of "the public" is a flaw, not in the societies we study, but in the manner in which we study them.

NOTES

1. Indeed, since Hobbes's *Leviathan*, "the public" exists only in the initial desire to end the "war of all against all," and in any crisis following the creation of the state, when the state is unable to protect its citizens. Once again, the public exists only at the moment of state creation (or re-creation, as the need arises), after which it disappears.

2. Erikson, Luttberg, and Tedin update this definition in a recent text: "the combined personal opinions of adults towards issues of relevance to government." (Erikson, et al., 1988:123)

3. By inference, the most important public decision outside of the perview of the state—the legitimization of the government itself—becomes impossible given this definition of public opinion. Conversely if a "public" separate from the state may legitimize the government, then the public realm must be defined without reference to the state.

4. See Riker and Ordeschook, 1968, for an example.

5. For an illustration and discussion of this point, see Barry and Hardin's example of a contentious political science department choosing a new chair (Barry and Hardin, 1982:216).

6. An initial response to this analysis might be that we know Procedure X to be the best system *only* for the express purpose of selecting among other decision systems. The problem with this argument is that it once again raises the question of how we gain this knowledge. If we can classify the use of particular decision procedures by some general rule, then it would be best to select a process for social decisions according to this rule, rather than by Procedure X.

7. Note that the above proof will also work when more than two decision systems are being evaluated.

2

The Dilemma Reconsidered: Opinion, Choice, and Public

The word "paradox" comes from the Greek *para* (beyond, contrary to) and *doxa* (opinion) and thus means etymologically "contrary to received opinion." It is thus quite similar to "unorthodox," though "orthodoxy" carries the sense of "right (or at any rate established) opinion" while *doxa* is neutral on this score (Barry and Hardin, 1982:373).

THE SPIRAL OF SILENCE

Recapturing the notion of "public" in public choice requires that we go beyond the notions of "public" in public opinion, as this term has tended to be defined. We discover the means to do so in the definition of public opinion provided by Elisabeth Noelle-Neumann's "spiral of silence" theory. This definition was outlined in detail in *The Spiral of Silence: Public Opinion—Our Social Skin* (1984).[1] Her theory describes the public realm as an arena in which one is exposed to the judgments of others and threatened with social isolation for unpopular positions. "Public opinion" becomes the opinions expressed in reaction to the fear of isolation, and "public" becomes a state of being, a feeling of exposure one feels in the presence of society's other members. This notion of public is quite different from the previous notions discussed with reference to public choice. Noelle-Neumann relegates the other definitions of the term to the first two out of "three meanings of public:"

... Many scholars have argued over the term "public" ... To begin with, there is the legal sense of "public" which emphasizes the etymological aspect of its *openness: it is open to everyone*—a public path, a public trial—as distinguished from the private sphere (from the Latin *privare*), or something distinguished or set aside as one's own. A second meaning can be found in the concepts of public rights and public force. Here "public" expresses some involvement of the state. ... *This means we are dealing with issues or problems that concern us all, that concern the general welfare.* States have the legalized use of force on this principle: *the single individual has surrendered the possibility of using force to the organs of the state.* (Noelle-Neumann, 1984:61; emphases mine)

Impossibility of exclusion, the general welfare, and legitimate decision-making powers or procedures—all three definitions from the public choice literature appear in these first two definitions of public. None of these definitions, however, is sufficient to capture the notion of public implied by Noelle-Neumann's definition of "public opinion."

The relevant "third meaning" of public as exposure to others' opinions is detailed in Noelle-Neumann's introduction to her concept of public opinion:

The third meaning of "public" could be described as social-psychological. The individual does not live only in that inner space where he thinks and feels. His life is also turned outside, not just to other persons, but also to the collectivity as a whole. Under certain conditions (I am thinking here of the famous distinction of Ferdinand Tönnies *Gemeinschaft* and *Gesellschaft*), the exposed individual is sheltered by the intimacy and trust engendered through, for example, a shared religion. In great civilizations, however, the individual stands exposed even more openly to the demands of society (Tönnies, 1922:69, 80). What is it that "exposes" the individual and continaully requires that he attend to the social dimension around him? It is fear of isolation, fear of disrespect and unpopularity; it is a need for consensus. This makes an individual want to focus his attention toward this anonymous court, which deals out popularity and unpopularity, respect and scorn.

Fascinated by the idea of the self-reliant, independent individual, scholars have barely noticed the isolated individual fearful of the opinions of his peers. (Noelle-Neumann, 1984:61–62)

Here, "public" refers to the individual's sense of "exposure" to the opinions and judgments of others, a feeling that one is operating in a realm where one risks being socially isolated. This description implies an interaction between the individual and the other members of the group or society. The individual is not only concerned with his private affairs; he is also concerned with the manner in which his actions are regarded by others. What is the nature of this feeling of "exposure" to others' opinions, and what are its implications for the formation of public opinion? As a means of addressing these questions, let us recall the problem that formed the stumbling block for public choice: individual choices could not be consistently aggregated to generate any of the notions of "public" endorsed by social choice theorists. Noelle-Neumann's definition describes how individual opinions become "public opinion," but this process goes beyond a simple tallying of individual opinions on a given issue. The transition from individual opinion to public opinion is a complex process, involving several steps that merit separate description and discussion.

Noelle-Neumann first distinguishes between the simple aggregation of individual opinions and public opinion, referring to the former as the "climate of opinion." This climate of opinion plays a key role in the creation of public opinion, through a process called the "spiral of silence." The two terms are not equivalent, as evidenced in this quotation: "The spiral of silence is a *reaction to* changes in the climate of opinion. The idea of a frequency distribution, of the relative strength of various contradictory tendencies is suggested more clearly by the expression 'climate of opinion' than by 'public opinion.' 'Climate' also brings to mind the image of time and place—something like Kurt Levin's notion of 'field' and climate also includes the most complete sense of public" (Noelle-Neumann, 1984:78–79; emphasis mine). Individuals' reactions to the "climate of opinion," or the distribution of individual opinions in the society, generate the notion of "public opinion." Noelle-Neumann isolates three steps toward a definition of "public opinion" in a given society:

. . . I have tried to identify elements that seem to be linked with the process of public opinion and are amenable to empirical investigation: (1) the human ability to realize when public opinions grow in strength or weaken; (2) *the reactions to this realization, leading either to more confident speech or silence*; and (3) *the fear of isolation that makes most people willing to heed the opinion of others*. It is on these three elements that an operational definition of public opinion may be built; opinions on controversial issues that one *can* express in public without isolating oneself. (Noelle-Neumann, 1984:62–63; emphases mine)

The author later expands this definition of public opinion, "for in the field of consolidated traditions, morals, and, above all, norms, the opinions and behaviors of public opinion are opinions and behaviors that one *must* express or adopt if one is not going to isolate oneself." (Noelle-Neumann, 1984:63)

The three steps described above form a process of public opinion when persons in the minority perceive their position lacks support. The "climate of opinion," or the simple aggregation of individual opinions, reflects the majority and minority positions on a given subject. Individuals who perceive themselves in the minority (at $t = t_1$) are less likely to voice their opinions. Their reluctance makes their position appear weaker, so that the perception that they are in the minority becomes even stronger (at $t = t_2$). The process continues in a circular fashion, with perception affecting public behavior (expression or silence) which, in turn, affects perception. The process resembles a "spiral" rather than a circle, however, because it occurs over time and because at each point (t_1, t_2, etc.) the position of the minority appears progressively weaker until it is virtually silenced (barring any drastic changes in the climate of opinion).

Individual opinion thus becomes "public opinion" only when its adherents sense that their position grows stronger in the population, and thus speak confidently with little fear of isolation. The elements of this theory are controversial and require separate discussion regarding their effects upon the notion of "public" in public choice. For if public opinion, so defined, precedes public choice, it must describe the parameters within which social choice operates.

PUBLIC EXPRESSION AND PUBLIC NOTICE

Let us being with an apparently self-evident proposition about collective choice:

Proposition I In order for a preference to be considered in collective decision making, that preference must be communicated in some manner.

Other theorists implicitly acknowledge this critical starting point for discussions of public choice. Barry devotes the first section of *Political Argument* to a discussion of language, assuming that desires that cannot be communicated in language cannot be evaluated as choices (Barry, 1965:2–3, 16–34).[2] Similarly, Kenneth Arrow notes that "Decisions, whenever taken, are a function of information received." He also states the converse: information that cannot be communicated (and hence, may not be received) can have no influence upon the decision (Arrow, 1984:168). The first proposition or theorem merely combines Professor Arrow's insight with his previous definition of public choice. The desires or preferences of "relevant group members" is the "information" needed for collective choice; preferences that are not communicated will not be part of the collective decision.

Public choice analysis departs from my present discussion regarding the distinction between individual preferences and publicly expressed individual preferences. Public choice analysts regard the two as equivalent, except under extreme circumstances that violate the spirit of "public choice." They generally assume that any individual preference that can be formulated in words will be expressed. The one caveat to this assumption occurs in strategic voting, in which persons deliberately misrepresent their private preferences in order to advance their overall interests (see Gibbard, 1973, for an example). In all cases, however, private interest drives and determines the expression of individual preferences in collective decision making.

This assumption is generally accepted because it is perceived that alternative assumptions do irreparable damage to the notion of responsive decision making (i.e. decision making based upon the individual preferences of group members). We tend to accept Arrow's condition of unrestricted domain (Arrow, 1963:24) in preference ordering and preference expression because we associate the exclusion of opinions with coercion. Examples of such exclusion easily come to mind. Coercion may be practiced by the state, or by groups or individuals within the society (as when terrorists attempt to silence "biased" reporting by kidnapping or assassinating journalists). Such examples carry us far afield from any notion of public choice based upon an "open market" of ideas and preferences. We therefore generally accept Barry and Hardin's assertion that even though unrestricted domain "may be factually irrelevant for . . . not all logically possible combinations of individual orderings will be displayed in a society," all possible orderings are *likely* to be expressed, given no other conditions than a finite number of alternatives and enough time (Barry and Hardin, 1982:215).

Public choice theorists would accept Proposition I as a self-evident precondition for an open society. According to Noelle-Neumann's theory, however, the issue is not so clear-cut, even in the most open societies. The next two propositions describe the complexity, and restrictiveness, of this first proposition.

MAJORITY OPINION AND SILENCING PROCESSES

The central theme of Noelle-Neumann's "spiral of silence" is that individuals tend to avoid expressing minority opinions due to the "fear of isolation." She assumes that this fear is a general motivation in human behavior, with effects profound enough to prevent individuals from speaking out against opinions contrary to their interests. Two critical questions thus arise concerning the effects of this motivation on public choice situations: Is this fear truly a general motivation that explains the public expression or silencing of opinions or preferences and does the discussion of this fear properly belong in analyses of public choice? Do we venture into the realm of vague (and immeasurable) motivations, which public choice theory was designed to avoid, when we speak of the fear of isolation? Obviously, we must answer the first question con-

cerning the pervasiveness of this motivation, before evaluating its usefulness in the present analysis.

Several studies have observed the "fear of isolation" by measuring its
effects upon public behavior; these studies include laboratory experiments and public opinion surveys. In one psychological experiment
performed by Solomon Asch in the early 1950s, respondents were asked
to match a standard line against three comparison lines; the correct
answer was obvious, and all ten participants correctly named the matching lines in successive tests (Noelle-Neumann, 1984:37–38). The experiment was then performed under different conditions; nine of the
participants were replaced by Asch's assistants, so that only the tenth
person was an actual respondent (who was unaware that the others
were assistants). The assistants all gave the same incorrect answer to
the matching. Sixty percent of the respondents followed suit, while 20
percent wavered in their evaluations, giving inconsistent answers. Only
20 percent of the respondents stuck to their original views, while often
explaining apologetically that they "always disagreed," or giving some
other indication that they felt uncomfortable in the position of odd person out (Asch, 1952:450–73). Noelle-Neumann ascribes the participants'
reactions to their awareness of potential isolation for their answers. She
notes that most individuals would have given an obviously wrong answer to avoid this feeling. Other studies by Milgram (1961:45–51; cited
in Noelle-Neumann, 1984:40) and Sherif (1935; 1966; cited in Glynn and
McLeod, 1985:48) yielded similar results using different techniques. In
each case, subjects "accepted the group norm, internalized it, and were
influenced by it long after the original situation" (Glynn and McLead,
1985:48).

But these experiments provide only preliminary evidence of the fear
of isolation as a general motivation. Two criticisms may be leveled at
these results. First, Noelle-Neumann's theory describes a process occurring over time, and involving effect and reinforcement; these experiments were one shot, or short-term, studies of single effects (Noelle-
Neumann, 1984:10). Noelle-Neumann's theory also assumes that the
degree of silencing varies with the strength of the threat of isolation
over time; this assumption is not tested adequately in these experiments.[3] Second, many social science researchers question the usefulness
of laboratory experiments for testing individuals' reactions to social situations; the laboratory experiment is too controlled, they argue, to justify
applying its conclusions to general social behavior.

An initial response to this last criticism is that it does not apply to
laboratory experiments per se, but rather to experiments used apart from
other means of studying social behavior. Indeed, the game theory experiments performed in laboratory testings form a critical part of public

choice theory (see Rappoport, 1982:18–34, for an example). Noelle-Neumann's analysis also addresses both criticisms by supplementing the laboratory tests with an array of creative survey research questions. One example concerns a "train test," where respondents' willingness to discuss controversial issues in a public situation was tested. On one survey, the people who believed it proper to smoke in front of nonsmokers (a minority position in the population) were asked if they would discuss this issue on a long train ride; the advocates of the right to smoke usually declined to do so. They were even more likely to decline a conversation when faced with an explicit threat of isolation, such as a hostile comment toward smokers voiced by a stranger during the ride. By contrast, nonsmokers (a clear majority of the population) were far less likely to be silenced by the prospect of a long train ride with strangers or hostile comments on their position (Noelle-Neumann, 1984:42–47).

The author obtains similar results by investigating other forms of social isolation. When respondents were asked to identify a party bumpersticker on a car with slashed tires, or a political button on a person treated rudely by a stranger, they tended to attribute these political symbols to the nation's less popular political party. Noelle-Neumann concludes that respondents viewed opponents of the popular position as candidates for social isolation (Noelle-Neumann, 1984:53–57). Furthermore, she notes that this view covaries with the popularity of the minority party; as the party became more popular, respondents were less likely to view its supporters as socially isolated. Glynn and McLeod obtain a similar result using data from the 1980 presidential contest in the United States; supporters of either Carter or Reagan were less likely to express their preferences in a nonsupportive social context than in a supportive context (Glynn and McLeod, 1985:57).

The evidence suggests that the fear of isolation generally motivates public expression or silencing of preferences. But is it proper to carry over these results into a discussion of preference expression in public choice? My preceding argument concerning the meaning of "public" suggested that this transfer might be a solution—and perhaps a necessary one—to the problem of adequately describing the content of public choice. There is, however, a theoretical and a methodological problem with this transfer. The theoretical problem is that motivations toward silencing may conflict with our other private interests; silencing may imply conceding our private interests to others' wishes (as suggested by Proposition I). Of course, in cases of simple majority rule involving only two choices, the point is moot. If the "fear of isolation" simply prevented the expression of minority opinions, the same outcome would result in a one-shot majority choice situation as when all opinions were expressed, albeit with a different proportion of assenting and dissenting votes. Beyond such simple choice operations, however, one quickly encounters conflicts between the motivation toward silencing and individuals' private interests, narrowly construed.

An initial response might be simply that considerations of silencing processes are nonetheless important and that these conflicts must be dealt with, even though they complicate our model somewhat. This is the response I wish to offer, remaining consistent with Noelle-Neumann's analysis—at no time does she state that individuals totally neglect their private interests to avoid isolation. If this were so, we would find ourselves in a peculiar state similar to the one described by Barry, in which individuals are so taken with the principle of majority choice that they wait upon others' preferences before they form their own (Barry, 1965:59–60). Obviously, the climate of opinion, which is formed of individual opinions, precedes public opinion. The actual problem here is methodological: can we operationalize the fear of isolation and the spiral of silence in a fashion rigorous enough to discuss their effects upon the individual and aggregate levels of public choice? I devote chapters 4 to 7 to this endeavor, but one must also defend the decision to proceed at this point, based upon a standard set for public choice analyses by Professor Barry.

We wish to avoid here the trap of "formalism," which Barry correctly criticizes in Downs's and Riker's analyses of voter motivations. Downs and Riker describe as a "reward" of voting the "satisfaction" one receives from the expressive act alone (Downs, 1957:267–71; Riker, 1968:28). Barry replies that "insofar as [this explanation] includes voting as a purely expressive act, not undertaken with any expectations of changing the state of the world, it fails to meet the minimum requirements of the means-end model of rational behavior" (Barry, 1978: 15). This criticism depends upon how one defines such terms as "means," "ends," and "rational behavior"; Barry notes that a virtue of social choice theory is that it endows these terms with definite, and rigorous, definitions based upon economic assumptions. As such, his criticism against Downs and Riker is not that they stray from "economic" assumptions, but rather that they do so in a vague and unsubstantiated manner. As he notes, the proper question is whether other motivations beyond narrow self-interest may be safely ignored when analyzing public choice situations (Barry, 1978:14–15). Barry thus presents two formidable challenges concerning our approach to social choice situations. First, does the spiral of silence theory allow us to move from behavioral premises to social activity in a rigorous manner? Noelle-Neumann's theory suggests that it does: we begin with an individual motivation (the desire to avoid isolation) and proceed from that motivation toward social actions designed to fulfill this end (expression or silencing of preferences). The decision to express or silence one's opinion is based upon the perception of whether that opinion is emerging as a majority or minority opinion, respectively. These tendencies have been investigated and verified by a variety of empirical tests.

We thus come to Barry's second challenge: while the spiral of silence may exist in social situations, may it be "safely ignored" in discussions of public choice? In a discussion of the spiral of silence and consumer behavior in chapter 5, I argue that it may not. This argument, which is based upon a critique of Fred Hirsch's *Social Limits to Growth*, is too detailed to summarize here, but it states basically that we cannot fully understand consumer behavior on the individual or aggregate levels if we ignore the effects of the fear of isolation. Barry argues that the "appropriateness" of the economic approach in public choice is based upon whether other factors may be excluded from this analysis; however, if one begins with economic assumptions, the spiral of silence theory is already implicitly included in the analysis. Barry's admonition should be viewed as a caution in discussions of public opinion and public choice, not as a prohibition of such discussion. With this challenge in mind, I advance Proposition II concerning the public expression of preferences:

Proposition II If an individual perceives he is in the minority, he is less likely to publicly express his opinion. This tendency toward public silence will increase the weaker the minority position is perceived to be, due to the increased fear of isolation (barring any changes in the underlying distribution of opinions). This process will continue until the minority opinion is virtually silenced.

THE COVARIANCE OF ACTUAL AND PERCEIVED OPINIONS

The amount and quality of information one has concerning individuals' preferences is a critical factor in most analyses of public choice. At least two volumes of Professor Arrow's collected papers are devoted to analyzing the place of information in economic and social decisions (Arrow, 1984; 1984a). Similarly, the amount of information voters have about others' intentions and preferences figures prominently in Downs's theory of the rationality of voting (Downs, 1957:260–71). Individuals' perceptions of changes in the strength of majority and minority opinions are similarly critical to Noelle-Neumann's analysis of public opinion, since the decision to express or silence one's opinion in public depends upon these perceptions. How does one obtain this information according to the spiral of silence theory? Noelle-Neumann states that individuals possess a "quasi-statistical sense" by which they can perceive whether an opinion is growing or declining in strength on a given issue, based upon their observations of the social environment (Noelle-Neumann, 1984:15).

We have already implied that individuals have some means of obtaining information about the strength of the majority and minority opinions. This knowledge prompts the transition between private opinions and public (or expressed) opinions. Yet, Noelle-Neumann's description of this sense still has a rather mysterious air about it for certain critics; indeed, the concept prompted one reviewer to dismiss her entire theory as dependent upon a vague and inadequately defined notion (see Hadari, 1985:213–14). But this notion is not as mysterious as the reviewer claims. Other disciplines in the social sciences—notably anthropology— have long assumed the existence of nonverbal means by which individuals in a given society send signals to one another concerning their opinions. Consider this description of how the distinction between "explicit" and "implicit" culture developed:

Both Freud and Sullivan drew heavily on the works of anthropologists—Freud indirectly, using anthropology to support his views, Sullivan in a more immediate way. Sullivan worked actively with the greatest descriptive linguist of our time, Edward Sapir, the man who laid the foundations for modern descriptive linguistics. While the psychologists were looking to anthropology to learn more about man as a social being, the anthropologists were using the theories of psychoanalysis in their attempts to formulate more satisfying theories of culture. One of the most significant of these borrowed theories was that culture existed on two levels: overt culture, which is visible and easily described, and covert culture, which is not visible and presents difficulties even to the trained observer ...When it soon turned out that this theory was inadequate to describe the cultural picture, anthropologists like Kluckhohn started speaking of explicit and implicit culture. Explicit culture, *Such things as law, was what people talk about and can be specific about.* Implicit culture . . . *was what they took for granted or what existed on the fringes of awareness.* (Hall, 1959:64–65; emphases mine)

There is a clear distinction made here between those characteristics, opinions, and values that one discusses publicly, and those that are not discussed or that "exist on the fringes of awareness," perceived by some inherent sense we possess as human beings. More recently, another anthropologist who has written extensively about "silencing processes" in societies took up this theme of the communication of values or opinions without benefit of language:

Communication systems are primarily associated in our minds with words. Nevertheless, it is by now well recognized, of course, that society has also devised many other symbolic codes. Of one, Edward Ardener has written: "We might visualize a semiotic system that depended, in the absence of the power of speech, upon the apperception by the human participants of contextually defined logical relations among themselves in space. Let us say: the relevant position of each participant to another in a gathering, and to items in a fixed environment" (1971, pp. xliii–iv). Thus, people may "jockey for position" knowing that their fellows may "read" from this their social importance. Thus, as Hall puts it, *space speaks.* (Ardener, 1981:12)

The appearance (and clear acceptance), in other social science disciplines, of the ability of individuals to perceive changes in the opinions and norms of others removes the mystery surrounding the quasi-statistical sense Noelle-Neumann describes. Yet, her description of this sense still requires empirical justification.

Noelle-Neumann's empirical proof that individuals can sense when an opinion gains or loses strength in a population rests upon the co-variance of individual opinions with the perceived majority opinion, when both are measured on the aggregate level. In one test, she asked respondents, first, if they favored or opposed the death penalty, and second, if "most people" favored or opposed the death penalty. When the aggregate responses to both questions were graphed together for an eight-month period, the results were striking—the percentage of favorable responses to both questions tended to covary over time. She obtained similar results using data on opposition to the death penalty, and voting intentions in West Germany and Great Britain (Noelle-Neumann, 1984:14–16). Glynn and McLeod obtained similar results in a more formal analysis, using data from the 1976 and 1980 American presidential elections (Glynn and McLeod, 1985:51–52).

The author concludes from these results that individuals are able to perceive when an opinion increases or decreases in support within a society. This conclusion has stimulated controversy, however. Other authors have claimed it as a statistical artifact arising from "looking glass perception." This alternative explanation states that individuals try to convince themselves of their position's legitimacy by ascribing their personal opinions to the majority (see Taylor, 1982:331–35). "Looking glass perception" is an intriguing response to Noelle-Neumann's findings, but it encounters empirical problems when examined. Noelle-Neumann notes that changes in individual views tend to be less dramatic than changes in perceptions of how others think. More importantly, estimates of how most people think change among supporters and opponents of this position (Noelle-Neumann, 1984:10–11). Individuals tend to display an uncanny ability to sense changes in the opinions of others in the population: "numerous sets of questions . . . consistently confirmed the people's apparent ability to perceive something about majority and minority opinions, to sense the frequency distribution of pro and con viewpoints, and this all quite independently of any published poll figures" (Noelle-Neumann, 1984:9–11).

The fact that analysts advance the "looking glass perception" explanation, however, does provide us with useful insights into the dynamics of opinion expression. For one must ask why an individual would claim that a majority supports his position without evidence to support this claim. It would not seem to advance my interests to claim that my opinion is supported by the majority in most cases. There seems to be no reason, for example, why I cannot state in August of 1986 that I do not approve of the manner in which Reagan is handling his job as president, while acknowledging that most Americans feel otherwise. The only plausible explanation why I might project my opinion onto the majority is that such a projection allows me to feel less alone—or less isolated—in my view. If the threat of isolation is strong enough to encourage this response, we have conceded that a major part of Noelle-Neumann's theory is correct.

This explanation is interesting, then, for the assumptions about human nature that it reveals. "Looking glass perception" implies that respondents wish to believe that a majority consensus favorable to their position exists in a society. It is thus a small step to assume that individuals will observe their social environment carefully to test whether others actually do concur with their opinions, in order to avoid isolation. This desire underscores the "desire for consensus" that Noelle-Neumann describes in her definition of "public." This desire will be discussed at length in the next section, when I consider the place of "societal indifference" in Noelle-Neumann's analysis. At this point, however, let us conclude with the third and final proposition derived from the spiral of silence theory:

Proposition III Individuals tend to perceive when a position is gaining or losing strength in the population. Hence, the sum of individual opinions, and the sum of perceived majority opinions, tend to covary over time.

THE SPECIAL CASE OF SOCIETAL INDIFFERENCE

Noelle-Neumann's theory concerns the conversion of individual opinions into public opinion, in situations where a clear majority opinion emerges in the society. But what occurs when no majority opinion emerges on an issue? How will individuals respond regarding expression or silencing of their opinions? First, it is seldom that individuals will not ascribe majority status to some opinion when asked; indeed, Noelle-Neumann notes that 80 to 90 percent of respondents are willing to give an evaluation of the climate of opinion on most issues. Indeed, the author notes that "even questions concerning the future of an opinion" tended to be answered by respondents (Noelle-Neumann, 1984:9).

The general problem in this case, then, is not whether individuals will tend to ascribe majority status to an opinion, but rather, what occurs in those special cases when there is no majority consensus emerging in the population. It is under these conditions that the threat of isolation has its greatest effect. When there is no clear majority emerging, individuals are generally unwilling to express their opinions for fear of isolating themselves. But if most people are afraid to express their opinions, then an undecided populace would appear to be an equilibrium point; as such, no consensus would ever emerge.

According to Noelle-Neumann's theory, a consensus does emerge because not all individuals are afraid to express their opinions due to the threat of isolation. Certain individuals are capable of ignoring their fear of isolation; by speaking out, these people define the emerging opinion. She divides these individuals into two groups: "heretics" and "opinion leaders." Both types are capable of introducing changes in public opinion; of the first group, Noelle-Neumann states:

Up to now, we have focused on people who are frightened or cautious, who fear isolation; now we shall look in the other direction, at those who do not fear isolation or are willing to pay its price—a more colorful group. These are people who introduce the new music; painters like Chagall, who, in a 1917 painting, *The Stable*, has a massive cow break through the roof of a house and peer out into the open; or scholars like John Locke, who claimed that men are hardly concerned with God's Commandments or the laws of the state. . . . In this circle we find the heretics, those human figures answering the needs of their time and yet timeless, who constitute the correlate to tightly united public opinion. . . . The relationship between conforming members and outsiders is not, however, to be understood only as an accentuation of the value system and the going rules of society by those who injure them and by their "exhibition" at the pillory.

The concept of the spiral of silence reserves the possibility of changing society to those who either know no fear of isolation or have overcome it. (Noelle-Neumann, 1984:139)

Individuals who are willing to speak out without fear of isolation are often ignored as a negligible portion of the population when public opinion is stable and a clearly dominant opinion exists. However, they have inordinate influence when opinions are in flux, for they create the impression that a dominant opinion is emerging by advocating a position when most others are afraid to declare their opinions. These individuals create the impression that a dominant opinion is emerging. This impression becomes a self-fulfilling prophecy as most individuals are willing to follow the expressed, or declared, opinion. It is for this reason that Noelle-Neumann claims there is an "advantage of having talkative groups on your side" (Noelle-Neumann, 1984:24) in a period of controversy, when the dominant opinion has not yet emerged.

The second group of individuals, the "opinion leaders," also introduce a means of resolving the supposed deadlock in the formation of public opinion. Unlike the heretics, these individuals are more in the mainstream of social life. These people are described by John Stuart Mills in *On Liberty*: "And what is a still greater novelty, the mass do not take their opinions from dignitaries in Church or State, from ostensible leaders, or from books. Their thinking is done for them by men much like themselves, addressing them or speaking in their name, on the spur of the moment. . . . " (Mill, in Noelle-Neumann, 1985:175).

"Opinion leaders" are distinguished from the rest of the population (people who tend to fear isolation, especially in times of controversy or crisis) by their peculiar attributes and motivations in social relationships. In her work on identifying opinion leaders, Noelle-Neumann describes the results of a factor analysis that measured the "strength of personality" displayed by certain individuals. She discovered that these "personality strength" measures allow researchers to identify opinion leaders in a society (Noelle-Neumann, 1985:212). These individuals are less concerned with disseminating a particular opinion because they derive pleasure solely from occupying the position of opinion leader. The following elements, presented as statements that respondents may accept or reject, make up the "strength of personality" scale for opinion leaders:

"I like to take the lead when a group does things together."

"I enjoy convincing others of my opinion."

"I like to assume responsibility."

"I often notice that I serve as a model for others."

"I am often a step ahead of others." (Noelle-Neumann, 1985:180)

Because individuals exist who derive pleasure from the mere act of leading public opinion, the undecided state in a society does not remain an equilibrium point. These people seek to resolve indifference by defining the dominant opinion that emerges. Even when these individuals are themselves initially divided, they will project an appearance of consensus, or early join an emerging consensus among other opinion leaders to retain their positions as opinion leaders. These persons are like the political candidates in Downs's analysis, who derive their rewards from advocating the dominant or emerging opinion, regardless of the content of that opinion (Downs, 1957:88). Because individuals exist who are willing to risk isolation for the psychic (or material) rewards of leading opinion, societal indifference does not tend to be an equilibrium point in public opinion. Individual opinions are always eventually transformed into public opinion in a society.

What are the results of removing "societal indifference" from the analysis? First, the idea that a society, as a decision-making entity, can be "indifferent" to two alternatives is a rather odd one for public opinion analysts. If we consider decision rules that are responsive to constituents' preferences, there are two conditions under which "societal indifference" may be an outcome in public choice. The first condition is if a decisive subset is indifferent between the alternatives offered, say x and *y*. For example, if decisions are made by majority rule, a majority states that it is indifferent to *x* and *y*, and this choice becomes part of the overall preference ordering. The second condition is if no alternative receives a decisive subset of votes—for example, if decisions are made by majority rule and no alternative receives a majority of votes.[4]

Let us consider the first example. Would we generally consider "indifference" to be an expression of public opinion on a subject? One would probably question instead what the "public" issue was concerning alternatives *x* and *y*, if either choice is equally acceptable to the society. The question's public nature is lost in situations of indifference. Put another way, public opinion deals with a society's preference on an issue, regardless of the manner in which that preference is determined. Is "indifference," on the individual level, really a preference? When I state "I prefer *x* to *y*," I am saying that I prefer *x* and not *y* out of this choice set. When I state that I am indifferent to *x* and *y*, I am stating that I have *no preference* in this matter. Indifference is the *absence of preference* on the issue. If a decisive subset of the population feels the same, the society is described as expressing an absence of preference on the issue. Decisions on the issue thus fall to private individuals, and the question is not a public issue (nor a suitable topic for public opinion).

Certain public choice theorists would disagree with this argument. They wish to use the condition of indifference in their formulation of decision rules for the society. Fishburn, for instance, wishes to rewrite Arrow's Pareto optimality condition to include a special case for indifference between alternatives. As Abrams describes this case:

Fishburn also shows that a reasonable *unanimity principle* can lead to a violation of the social transitivity condition. . . . Recall that . . . the Pareto principle was defined as follows: if xP_iy for all *i*, then xPy. That is, if everyone prefers *x* to *y*, *x* must be the social preference. The *unanimity principle* is somewhat different. It says if xR_iy for all *i*, and if xP_iy for some *i*, then xPy. That is, if no one prefers *y* to *x* (which is another way of saying that if everyone prefers either *x* to *y* or is indifferent between *x* and *y*) and if at least one individual prefers *x* to *y*, then *x* should be the social preference in a contest between *x* and *y*. (Abrams, 1980:74)

Fishburn builds the notion of individual indifference directly into the rules that determine social outcomes. This formulation does appear reasonable. But it does not indicate the importance of individual and social indifference in public opinion. For the rule appears reasonable because it relies upon an implicit change in the preference orderings of the individuals involved. The justification of this rule may be stated as such: "Since most people do not care if *x* or *y* is the alternative, and a passionate minority (or some other less than decisive subset of the population) desires one alternative, we will let them have their way." This justifi-

Figure 1
Example of a polarized distribution of opinion

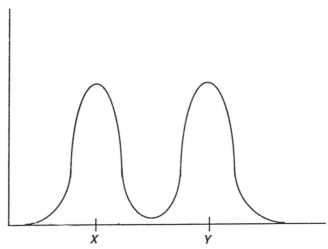

cation implies that those persons who were formerly indifferent change their decision, and state a preference ordering of x over y, in deference to the minority's wishes. Fishburn's rule thus seems reasonable because it rests, not upon the inclusion of individual indifference in the decision process, but upon the expectation that indifferent individuals will change their minds and prefer the alternative desired by the minority. The rule ultimately rests upon individual preferences, not individual indifference, between the choices.

Let us now consider the second case in which "societal indifference" may result. Here, no alternative achieves a decisive subset of votes, according to the decision rule being used. Public opinion analysts would not describe this condition as "societal indifference." Instead, it would be a case of "societal polarization," in which no decision-making consensus could emerge. Consider the classic example of an opinion distribution in society like the one shown in Figure 1. It would be difficult to argue that this opinion distribution describes an equilibrium state, even if neither mode represented a decisive subset according to the decision rule used. Including "societal indifference" in an overall preference ordering based upon this opinion distribution is an odd assumption. In this case also, the notion of societal indifference seems of little descriptive use in public opinion analysis. As a result, it is also of little use in public choice analysis.

CONCLUSION

It is now useful to take stock of where we are. We have derived three propositions from the spiral of silence theory that effect the transition of individual opinions into public opinion. Through the processes described in these theorems (and the accompanying arguments), a sense of public arises out of individuals' private opinions in a society. But now we must return to the question that prompted this incursion into Noelle-Neumann's theory: is this definition of "public" sufficient to define the realm in which public choice operates?

This question should be stated in a broader, and more useful, fashion: *does public opinion, as we have described and operationalized it here, generate the consensus (or the sense of "public") that makes "public choice" possible in a society?* In order for public opinion to accomplish this task, the desired theorems must provide reasonable solutions for the three stumbling blocks that hindered the definition of "public" in the first place—the Arrow problem, the problem of collective action, and the problem of legitimizing choice procedures responsive to constituents' preferences. In the rest of the book I will argue that public opinion, as operationalized by the three propositions in this chapter, accomplishes this task on general and specific levels. Chapter 3 will describe the linkages between these three problems on the axiomatic level, so that the theorems may be applied as a general solution. All three problems are indeed "paradoxes" in the truest sense implied by the quotation at the head of this chapter—they are contrary to (public) opinion, which effects their resolution, making public choice possible in a society.

NOTES

1. The German edition, entitled *Die Schweigespirale*, appeared in 1980.
2. See especially Barry's quotation from Ramsey: "what we can't say we can't say, and we can't whistle it either;" (Barry, 1965:3).
3. Preliminary evidence from other experiments seems to verify that the percentage of individuals giving the incorrect answer does tend to covary with the percentage of persons in the group who give that answer, however. My students were fascinated by the Asch results, but wished to test Noelle-Neumann's assumptions even further by repeating the experiment under slightly different conditions. In their version, the percentage of incorrect opinions was varied, so that it represented a minority view in some tests and a majority view in other tests. They expected that the larger the majority of persons who expressed the incorrect view, the more likely the actual respondent was to express the incorrect view. They also expected that when the incorrect response was clearly a minority view, that the actual respondents should have been likely to express the correct choice. The results verified their expectations; it was only when the incorrect choice was a *clear* majority opinion that it began to affect the respondents' expression of the correct answer. This effect upon the respondents also increased as the size of the majority increased.
4. There is some controversy over whether the latter case should be considered an instance of societal indifference or societal indecisiveness. The distinction is important, for the latter violates one of the conditions in Arrow's General Possibility Theorem, while the former does not. The two terms may also not be

used interchangeably, as they are not equivalent in meaning. I discuss some of the problems that arise with these definitions in the following chapter. At present, I consider the situation where no alternative receives a decisive subset of votes as a *possible* condition of societal indifference, for those who wish to classify it as such.

3

Arrow's Proof and Collective Action

While there is general agreement that the problems described in the last chapter define major issues in the field of public choice, little has been done to describe the underlying linkages between these problems. Abrams, in the conclusion of his book on social choice, does provide a matrix that compares the various problems of this subfield, including two of the three discussed earlier (Abrams, 1980:330–31). In many ways, however, this discussion is dedicated more to highlighting the differences between the problems than discussing the ways in which they are related. A classic exception is Hardin's work on the link between the Prisoners' dilemma and the problem of collective action (Hardin, 1971, 1982). Hardin's work added a new dimension to public choice literature by illustrating the usefulness of studying the relationship between these problems on a general level.

In this chapter, I integrate the public choice literature further by arguing that the Arrow problem, the problem of collective action, and the problem of legitimizing responsive choice procedures all follow from the same axiomatic principles. As such, they imply a similar solution, which will be advanced in chapter 4. This solution lies in the theorems, or propositions, I derived from Noelle-Neumann's theory in the last chapter. Before turning to this argument, however, it is necessary to illustrate the three problems' common roots.

This argument has two parts. First, I define a typology of rules and prove that Arrow's problem involves a conflict between two different axiomatic principles for which there is no solution short of eliminating one of the principles, or changing the axiomatic status of both rules. Second, I demonstrate that the Prisoners' dilemma and the problem of collective action are both special cases of the Arrow theorem, and thus imply a similar solution. This solution is introduced in chapter 4 when I discuss how the three theorems derived earlier promote democracy as a privileged decision rule.

A TYPOLOGY OF DECISION RULES

The typology of decision rules rests upon two binary distinctions. The first distinguishes privileged from nonprivileged rules. As stated in chapter 1, any procedure used to choose decision rules must be a privileged choice as an outcome. If the decision system consists of only one such axiomatic rule, then that rule is a privileged rule. If the decision system consists of two or more separate rules, then those rules are nonprivileged rules. In practice, these rules have different domains:

Definition 1a   A *privileged* rule determines the outcome in a collective decision, regardless of other rules that may exist.

Definition 1b   A *nonprivileged* rule either determines the outcome in a collective decision, or blocks the outcomes that result from other rules that may exist.

These qualities derive from the rules' origins. If a decision system contains only one rule, then that rule must be the best possible means for making choices, according to the Rule of Privileged Choice. It would be irrational to allow another rule to override it; privileged rules must always determine the outcome of a decision. The situation is more complex with nonprivileged rules. If a decision system contains two or more separate rules, then this set of rules must be better than any other possible rules (or they would not be used for choices) and be of equal value for decision making, when compared with one another (since less valuable rules would be eliminated in favor of better rules). The former demand explains why nonprivileged rules constitute the decision system. The latter demand explains why nonprivileged rules must prevail in a decision, or block each others' outcomes. If all nonprivileged rules yield the same outcome within the decision system, then this result must prevail. If the rules yield different outcomes, however, the decision system provides no means to decide between outcomes (since both rules are of equal value for decision making). Multiple outcomes block a decision.

From these definitions, a decision system may have only one privileged rule. Assume that a decision system has two privileged rules, X

and Y. Either the two rules always yield the same outcome, or the two rules may yield conflicting outcomes. If the two rules always yield the same outcome, then they are the same rule, albeit with different names; at least, we may not prove that they are separate rules. If the two rules yield different outcomes, then one rule must override the other, or both decisions will be blocked. If one rule, say X, overrides the other, then X is the privileged rule. If neither rule overrides the other, so that both decisions are blocked, then the two rules are nonprivileged, and neither rule is privileged.

A possible response to this analysis is "But what if there are certain cases in which X applies, and certain cases in which Y applies? Could both rules not be 'privileged' rules under these circumstances?" If we assume that we know which rules apply in which cases (as when we define our rules for going to work by saying "On Monday, Wednesday, and Friday I use Main Street, while on Tuesday and Thursday I use North Street"), then we are not talking about two separate rules. Instead, we are talking about one rule (here, a rule used to decide my route to work), which is made up of several parts, none of which conflict. These conclusions lend a perspective to a comment made by Barry concerning John Stuart Mill's reflections on decision rules. Mill asserts that all decisions must be reducible to one final rule or principle (Mill, 1956:620–21). Barry argues that there may be two or more rules for a given decision (Barry, 1965:4). This argument actually turns on terminology. There may be only one privileged rule, and Mill's statement is correct for decision systems governed by such a rule. But Barry is correct in that there may be two (or more) nonprivileged rules determining a decision.[1]

The second step in establishing the typology of rules distinguishes rules that are responsive from rules that are doctrinaire. This distinction draws its inspiration from two different sources. One source is Lindblom's distinction between Model 2 and Model 1 decision systems, respectively, from *Politics and Markets* (Lindblom, 1978:250). As Lindblom defines both systems:

In Model 1, since people know how to organize a society, the test of an institution is that it is correct. . . . in Model 2, people are not competent to know what is correct, [so instead] they fall back on their volitions, however imperfectly known, as a test. . . .
Suppose a society of three people wants to decide which restaurant to go to for dinner. In the style of Model 1, it would study the question on the assumption that there exists one correct solution discernible by diagnosis. In the style of Model 2, it would look for a process or interaction to make analysis necessary. . . . It might take a vote. . . . Or negotiate a decision, letting each of the three bring persuasion or other influences to bear on the others. (Lindblom, 1978:250–53)

Since we are not yet interested in decision systems, but rather in classifying the general rules underlying these systems, let us reduce Lindblom's distinctions to these rules. If a rule is based upon some combination of all individuals' preferences or volitions, then it is a responsive rule. If a rule is based upon some "correct" principle that need only be applied to the problem, then it is a *doctrinaire* rule. These rules have different implications when applied:

Definition 2a   A *responsive* rule requires that the individual preferences of persons in the group be known before an outcome may be reached.

Definition 2b   A *doctrinaire* rule requires that the governing principle for the decision be known before an outcome may be reached.

The typology of rules is generated out of the four possibilities afforded by these two binary distinctions. A rule may be privileged and responsive, privileged and doctrinaire, nonprivileged and responsive, or nonprivileged and doctrinaire. I am assuming here that this typology of rules is exhaustive with respect to the classification of responsive and doctrinaire rules. One might argue that there are other methods of deciding outcomes that do not rely upon citizen volitions or defined principles for judgment. Indeed, Barry avoids this problem by referring to responsive rules as "want-regarding" and all other rules as "ideal-regarding" (Barry, 1965:38–41). A rule that orders social preferences by chance (such as a lottery) would be one example in which the rule is doctrinaire (since it does not require knowing individual preferences for application), but where there is no set principle for ordering. I will deal with this case briefly later. My analysis of Arrow's proof applies using either of these interpretations of responsive or doctrinaire rules. However, I still tend to favor the more restrictive classification of decision rules implied by Lindblom's categories.

A few characteristics of these rules are worth noting. First, a privileged and responsive rule may yield only one unique outcome. Let us consider the result if this were not the case. Assume that there are several outcomes possible using a given responsive rule based upon individual preferences. This situation might arise if, for instance, one-third of a given group was needed to decide an outcome. In this case, we could apply the rule three times and obtain three different outcomes in a group evenly split between three alternatives. Our rule would provide no means of deciding between these outcomes—hence, the rule would be nonprivileged with respect to itself. If a responsive rule cannot produce a unique choice from among a set of preferences, it cannot be privileged.

The distinction between responsive and doctrinaire rules does not affect this conclusion; privileged and doctrinaire rules must also produce unique outcomes, due to the reasons described above. For this reason, rules that order outcomes by chance selection are nonprivileged (with respect to themselves) because the rule may be applied several times to the same choice set with different results. Put another way, chance selection rules may not be a privileged choice as a decision system, since chance selection requires that more than one alternative be a possible choice. If more than one alternative is not possible as an outcome, the process is not a chance selection; if more than one alternative is possible, the process cannot be privileged by the Rule of Privileged Choice.

Rules that are privileged and doctrinaire, however, have other special implications. A person who invokes such a rule need not consult with any other members of the group in order to prevail in a social decision. He is, in Arrow's terms, a dictator, or more correctly, a *privileged dictator*. Recall Arrow's definition of a dictator—an individual whose preference for x over y becomes the social choice, regardless of others' preferences (Arrow, 1963:30). Doctrinaire rules, by definition, do not consider preferences in determining outcomes; hence, any person who invokes a privileged and doctrinaire rule must prevail, regardless of others' preferences. Conversely, Arrow's dictator may not exist without a rule that is privileged and doctrinaire. If the rule is nonprivileged and doctrinaire, the individual may block all decisions other than the one he prefers, but he may not be able to prevail, as required by Arrow's definition. If the rule is responsive (and either privileged or nonprivileged), other individuals' preferences are already included in the calculation of a social choice.[2] This conclusion lends perspective to Little's argument that we are all dictators with regards to moral decisions (Little, 1982:278). Insofar as we make moral decisions based upon principles and not upon others' preferences, Little is correct. We follow a privileged and doctrinaire rule in this instance.

As a final note, nonprivileged rules are of interest because their presence is implied whenever a decision is blocked by the conflict of two or more equally valued rules. Outcomes may be only blocked by the conflict of nonprivileged rules (since privileged rules must always prevail). If manipulability of outcomes depends upon stalemate, as Gibbard (1973) claims, then stalemate depends upon the existence of nonprivileged rules.

The typology of decision rules will be used next to describe the underlying assumptions in Arrow's problem and the problem of collective action. For Arrow sets before the reader the impossible task of describing conditions under which two different privileged rules may coexist within the same decision system.

ARROW'S PROOF: AN EXAMINATION OF
TWO-CHOICE SETS

Early on in *Social Choice and Individual Values*, Arrow presents the problem of cyclical group preferences, using the example of cyclical majorities (Arrow, 1963:3). Of course, Arrow's proof goes far beyond the boundaries of the example of intransitive group preferences under majority rule. But this beginning point obscures the axiomatic bases of Arrow's problem. The general reason why Arrow's proof works has little to do with the specific problem of cyclical group preferences. The cycle is merely one counterexample—albeit a striking and important one, as I will discuss later—which illustrates the impossibility of Arrow's problem. Arrow himself makes no other claim for this specific example (Arrow, 1963:59). I will illustrate the impossibility of Arrow's task by using only two alternatives, x and y, and the general types of rules implied by Arrow's five conditions.

The Arrow problem states that no responsive decision system may meet all of five "reasonable conditions" for decisionmaking. These conditions have been stated in many forms by Arrow (1963), Plott (1982), Barry and Hardin (1982), and others and may be summarized in the following ways:[3]

1. Condition (O) (the social welfare function): The decision process or rule must generate *one and only one* ordering of possible social states, based upon individual orderings of these states, where each person is allowed one social ordering as input into the process. This condition includes Arrow's Axiom II, which states that the social ordering be transitive over preference or indifference.[4]

2. Condition (U): The social ordering must produce a unique outcome for all logically possible individual orderings of social states.

3. Condition (D) (nondictatorship): No person may exist whose preference for one alternative over another prevails without regard for others' preferences.

4. Condition (P) (Pareto optimality): If everyone prefers x to y, then x is preferred to y in the final social ordering.

5. Condition (I) (Irrelevant alternatives): Let S equal any subset of alternative social states in X. The final social ordering of any alternatives in S may only be affected by the individual orderings of alternatives in S. If individuals reorder alternatives not included in S, the final ordering of alternatives in S must remain the same as before the rearrangement of these other irrelevant alternatives.

Let us consider the implications of these conditions in the following order: (D), (U), (I), (P), and (O), for a two-choice set consisting of x and y.

Condition (*D*) disallows privileged dictators. Recall that if a privileged and doctrinaire rule exists, then a privileged dictator may exist. Hence, condition (*D*) is *sufficient* to disallow such rules. But this condition has broader implications: if a privileged dictator may exist, then there must be a rule that is privileged and doctrinaire for this individual to invoke (by my argument in the previous section). If no such rule exists, condition (*D*) is implied. Condition (*D*) is thus *necessary and sufficient* to disallow privileged and doctrinaire rules.

Condition (*U*) implies that nonprivileged rules may not exist. A nonprivileged rule may have its outcome blocked by another nonprivileged rule, for a given set of preferences. If there are nonprivileged rules, it follows that there is a set of preferences for which the decision rule does not produce an outcome—if nonprivileged rules exist => not (*U*) must be true. Condition (*U*) is *sufficient* to disallow nonprivileged rules. Note that privileged rules that always prevail by definition (and which therefore produce an outcome in each case) are compatible with condition (*U*). This condition is therefore compatible with the existence of a dictator.

The implications of condition (*I*) are somewhat more complex. Assume the opposite of (*I*) for a two-choice set, [*x*, *y*]. "Not (*I*)" implies that the individual orderings of *x* and *y* are the same in S and S', but the social ordering of *x* and *y* is different in the two sets. Assuming that S and S' are identical in their individual orderings of *x* and *y*, even while S and S' are drawn from different sets of alternatives, we may assume S = S' regarding *x* and *y*. We have derived two possible outcomes from a given set of preferences using the same rule; the rule is nonprivileged with respect to itself. This conclusion also holds if a doctrinaire rule is used, since the dictator prevails in one ordering but not in the other. If we assume "not (*I*)" then we may have nonprivileged rules. If we may not have nonprivileged rules, then condition (*I*) applies. Condition (*I*) is *necessary* to disallow nonprivileged rules.

What of condition (*P*), however? The implications of condition (*P*) are more extensive than the implications of the other rules. I will divide this discussion into two parts. First, let us define the opposite of (*P*): "not (*P*)" states that if all prefer *x* to *y*, *x* is *not* preferred to *y* in the overall social ordering. What are the implications of this negation of (*P*)?

If all individuals prefer *x* to *y*, then *x* is preferred to *y* by a subset of any size within the group. Since the social choice is "not *xPy*" (or not "where *x* is preferred to *y* by the group"), no subset is decisive for *x* over *y* based upon members' preferences. A rule that is privileged and responsive requires a decisive subset's existence; such a rule may not exist under these circumstances. Similarly, if all prefer *x* to *y*, then a privileged dictator, as a member of the group, also prefers *x* to *y*. Since *x* is not preferred to *y* as the social choice, however, a privileged dictator does not exist. Because such a person may not exist, a privileged and doctrinaire rule may not be used for decision making.

May the decision rule be nonprivileged under these circumstances? Neither a responsive nor a doctrinaire privileged rule may exist under the condition of "not (P)." If either of these types of rules is nonprivileged, however, they may block an outcome and theoretically reach the result of "not xPy." But each of the rules would still require an outcome to block. That outcome could not result from a responsive rule, because if all prefer x to y, and xPy is not the social choice, then there are no decisive subsets and no responsive rules. Similarly, that outcome could not result from a doctrinaire rule because if all prefer x to y, and xPy is not the social choice, there are no potential dictators, and no doctrinaire rules. Nonprivileged rules thus may also not exist under the condition of "not (P)."[5]

None of the rules in the typology may exist under a condition of "not P." Because the typology of decision rules is exhaustive, if any decision rule exists $=> (P)$. The converse of this conclusion is also true. If condition (P) holds, then the rule may be responsive (since any sized subset will be decisive when all are agreed) or doctrinaire (since the privileged dictator must be decisive if all, including him, are agreed). Since under condition (P), a rule will be invoked and prevail (given no dissenters to the social choice), the rule may be privileged or nonprivileged. Thus, (P) is compatible with all four types of rules—if $(P) => $ any of the rules may exist. (P) is a *necessary and sufficient* condition for all decision rules.

As a second point, consider the conflicts that occur when two rules yield conflicting outcomes. First, if there are two or more rules that conflict, they cannot be privileged because neither rule may override the other. The nonprivileged rules that remain may be divided into those rules with no indifference points (i.e. conditions under which the group is indifferent between alternatives), those rules whose indifference points coincide, and those rules whose indifference points do not coincide. If a rule has no indifference points in application, but conflicts with other nonprivileged rules that have no indifference points, then those conflicts may be considered as indifferent outcomes. Similarly, if all the nonprivileged rules have the same indifference points, then any conflicts that occur between outcomes may also be considered indifference. In both cases, however, we are not talking about separate rules; the nonprivileged rules are not blocking outcomes (since societal indifference is an outcome) where they do not prevail. We must combine these rules into one privileged rule, or the rules may not exist (since they would not be privileged or nonprivileged).

If the nonprivileged rules have different indifference points, then there must arise some instance where one rule, say rule A, yields an outcome of xPy or yPx, while another rule, say rule B, yields indifference between

x and y as an outcome. But here we cannot define this conflict as indifference; since A yields a preferential outcome and B yields indifference, rule B prevails over rule A if we interpret the conflict as indifference. But rules A and B are both nonprivileged; hence, rule B cannot prevail over rule A.

If we interpret conflicts between two separate rules as societal indifference, then those rules may not be privileged or nonprivileged. No rules may exist under these conditions. Since (P) implies that any rule may exist, however, if no rule may exist $=>$ not (P). Interpreting a conflict between separate rules as group indifference must violate condition (P).[6]

Condition (P) also implies condition (U). If "not (P)" $=>$ there are no decision rules. But if there are no decision rules $=>$ not (U), for we have no means of reaching a decision. If condition (U) applies, then condition (P) also applies.

It is useful to summarize our conclusions thus far. Each of the four conditions we have discussed has different implications for the typology of decision rules:

1. Condition (D) is *necessary and sufficient* to eliminate rules that are privileged and doctrinaire ($D <=>$ no rules are privileged and doctrinaire).
2. Condition (U) is *sufficient* to eliminate nonprivileged rules of any kind ($U =>$ no rules are nonprivileged).
3. Condition (I) is *necessary* to eliminate nonprivileged rules of any kind (no rules are nonprivileged $=> I$).
4. Condition (P) is *necessary and sufficient* for the existence of any type of rule ($P <=>$ any of the types of rules may exist). (P) is also *sufficient* to disallow interpreting the conflict between two separate rules as indifference ($P =>$ conflicts between separate rules are not equivalent to group indifference).

Let us now consider the transitive property of condition (O). If a rule is responsive, then by definition we must know individual preferences to apply it. Conversely, if we must know individual preferences to apply a rule, then the rule is responsive. If transitivity holds, we need not know individual preferences—only group preferences—to apply it. Hence, transitivity is not a responsive rule; it may be privileged and doctrinaire, or nonprivileged and doctrinaire. If the former, then no responsive rule may exist; if the latter, then nonprivileged and responsive rules may exist. The transitive condition is necessary and sufficient to eliminate privileged and responsive rules. We thus arrive at our final conclusion regarding Arrow's five conditions for decision rules:

5. Condition (O)'s transitive condition is *necessary and sufficient* to eliminate rules that are privileged and responsive (transitive condition $<=>$ no rules are privileged and responsive).

Note that I have used the less restricted definition of doctrinaire rules in the above statements. I have shown that the transitive rule must be doctrinaire because it cannot be responsive. This usage is consistent with Barry's definition of "ideal-regarding" principles as those principles that are not "want-regarding." Let us now consider the more restricted definition of doctrinaire rules implied by Lindblom's classification: doctrinaire rules are rules that demand the application of a given principle, or standard, for deciding between alternatives. If this definition is used, then we may go beyond stating that transitivity is doctrinaire because it is not responsive. We may state that transitivity is compatible (and indeed, implied) by all rules that are privileged and doctrinaire, except those doctrinaire rules that order outcomes by chance, such as lotteries. These rules are nonprivileged and doctrinaire. I would argue, however, that doctrinaire rules that rely upon chance rather than set principles to order outcomes are odd, and hence uninteresting, exceptions to the more restrictive classification inspired by Lindblom's models. If by a given principle or standard, x is preferred to y, and y is preferred to z, then x must be preferred to z according to rankings on this standard. Arrow concedes that group choices will always be transitive if the group ranks alternatives according to the same principle (Arrow, 1963:74–91). Following the more restricted definition of doctrinaire rules, if the rule is privileged and doctrinaire $=>$ transitivity *must* be true. The general conclusion also holds in this circumstance; the transitive condition is still necessary and sufficient to eliminate rules that are privileged and responsive. Throughout the rest of the book, I will tend to use the more restricted definition of doctrinaire rules implied by Lindblom's categories. But I will also insure that my conclusions are compatible with the less restricted definition implied by Barry's categories.

It is now clear why the task Arrow describes is impossible: his five conditions systematically eliminate rules that are privileged and doctrinaire, nonprivileged, and privileged and responsive. Since these conclusions exhaust all categories of my typology of rules, no decision rule may simultaneously meet all five conditions. But have we advanced our understanding of Arrow's problem, or merely restated it? I will argue briefly for the former by demonstrating how the typology of rules explains the mechanics of Arrow's proof and predicts the problems encountered by proposed solutions to the Impossibility Theorem.

PROPOSED SOLUTIONS

Let us begin with my original statement that Arrow's proof has little to do specifically with the problem of cyclical preferences. However, the cycle is central to the manner in which Arrow proceeds. Consider an alternative view of the proof, in terms of the described typology of rules.

Arrow's proof proceeds in two parts. The first part shows that having a dictator is compatible with conditions (U), (I), (O), and (P). The second part shows that meeting these conditions is *only* compatible with allowing a dictator to exist, thus violating condition (D). These two parts may thus be combined into one logical statement, using my classification of rules: having a rule that is privileged and doctrinaire (and hence, allowing a dictator), is necessary and sufficient for meeting conditions (U), (I), (O), and (P).

The first part of this proof follows easily from conclusions (1) through (5) above. A privileged and doctrinaire rule is sufficient to meet condition (O)'s demand for transitive social orderings (in this case, because transitivity is the privileged and doctrinaire rule). It also meets conditions (U) and (I), which are necessary and sufficient to eliminate nonprivileged rules, but not privileged ones. Finally, it meets condition (P), since any rule out of the typology will meet this condition.

In the second part of Arrow's proof, transitivity disallows any rule that is privileged and responsive. Such a rule may meet conditions (U), (I), and (P), but it may not meet condition (O)'s demand for transitive group preferences. Transitivity may be guaranteed *if and only if* the rule is privileged and doctrinaire. Since such a rule is a necessary and sufficient condition for a dictator's existence, transitivity of group preferences is true if and only if a dictator may exist. Arrow illustrates this point by the counterexample of cyclical preferences; I illustrate this point by logical negation based upon my classification of rules. The result is the same in either case—one must violate condition (D).

We have pursued Arrow's proof on a more general level here, in part because we have used only two alternatives, x and y, to derive the effects of his conditions. Of course, one could argue that we cannot actually discuss transitivity without a third alternative. But this argument obscures the usefulness of my approach. Once we have classified rules in terms of the typology described above, we may predict where irresolvable conflicts between conditions will occur. These predictions can help determine where the contradiction occurs and to judge which conditions should be relaxed (if any) within the decisionmaking process at a given point. In the general case of Arrow's proof, any rule that is privileged and doctrinaire cannot meet condition (D), while any condition that is not privileged and doctrinaire cannot meet condition (O). The other conditions eliminate the possibility of allowing decisions to be blocked. This conclusion will hold for rules dealing with two or more alternatives; Arrow's use of three alternatives is necessary because he proceeds by counterexample in his proof. But it is the genus of rules to which transitivity conforms which creates the contradiction; one need only find a counterexample which illustrates this contradiction.

It is useful to pursue a few variations on this theme. First, let us note that a rule which is privileged and responsive will meet conditions (*D*), (*U*), (*I*), and (*P*), but not condition (*O*); this result follows from conditions (1) through (5) above. If majority rule is a privileged rule, then, it will meet the first four of Arrow's conditions. May proves this point without reference to the typology of rules (May, 1982:199–203).

A second variation concerns another set of proposed "solutions" to Arrow's problem. These proposals include interpreting the conflict between outcomes of two rules as indifference, or creating additive rules that produce indifferent results for cyclical preferences. Both strategies proceed in a similar manner; the conflict between two separate decision rules yields an indifferent result. I have shown above that if there are two separate rules, each rule must be nonprivileged; hence, conditions (*U*), (*I*), and (*P*) will be violated. Critics who have discovered these violations have tended to be guided by creative intuition in searching out relevant and striking counterexamples to the solutions. Let us retrace their work, making predictions on the violations they will discover, based upon conclusions (1) through (5).

Consider first the situation described by Plott in which there are four alternatives, and three persons choosing between them (Plott, 1982:234). Assume the preference orderings are as follows:

first person: $yP_1x_1PwP_1z$

second person: $xP_2wP_2zP_2y$

third person: $wp_3zP_3yP_3x$

Plott uses this preference ordering to consider the possibility of interpreting a conflict between two decision rules—transitivity and majority rule—as indifference. From conclusion (4), this interpretation should violate condition (*P*). Plott proves this point by counterexample; he suggests we consider the paired choices in the following order: [*w,x*], [*x,y*], [*y,z*]. By applying majority rule to the pairs, and transitivity to the resulting group preferences, one obtains the result *zPw*. By applying majority rule to one pair, [*w,z*], one obtains the result *wPz*. Interpreting this conflict between the two rules as indifference, yields the result *zIw*; but since all persons prefer *w* to *z*, this outcome violates condition (*P*). If we assume that both majority rule and transitivity are nonprivileged rules, then the two results block each other; there is no outcome in the process. But if there is no outcome, then *wPz* is not the result, even though all prefer *w* to *z*. Once again, we violate condition (*P*).

What are the other alternatives? Although Plott does not consider demoting the rules to nonprivileged status, one may just accept that no decision may be reached between *w* and *z*, even though this violates

(P). This conclusion violates condition (U). If one concludes that a different result is derived from the same preference orderings, depending upon the order in which pairs of alternatives are considered, condition (I) is violated. As predicted, all of these interpretations, which operate by demoting the responsive rule and transitivity to nonprivileged status, run afoul of conditions (P), (U), and (I), as by conclusions (2) through (4) above.

Let us consider another alternative, the Borda rule. Plott proves by counterexample that this additive rule violates condition (I). In fact, it also violates condition (U), and can run afoul of condition (P), since it demands that the additive rule and transitivity be nonprivileged.

The Borda rule begins in a clever fashion. The rule is constructed so that cyclical preferences generate an indifferent outcome. Hence, if x, y, and z are part of the cycle, the rule's result is $xIyIz$. The problem with this solution is that the conflict underlying Arrow's proof has nothing specifically to do with cyclical preferences; these preferences are merely the counterexample used to illustrate the impossibility of the task Arrow defines. Put another way, the conflict between two rules is not dependent upon the specific location of either rule's indifference point, as shown in my proof of (4). If the rules are genuinely separate—and any responsive and transitive rules must be separate given all possible preference configurations—then the two rules must be nonprivileged. We violate conditions (U) and (I).

To illustrate this point, recall the description of the Borda rule. For my example, I will use the classic case of cyclical preferences among persons ranking three alternatives:

	A	B	C
first choice:	x	y	z
second choice:	y	z	x
third choice:	z	x	y

By the Borda rule, a person's first choice receives three points, his second choice receives two points, and his third choice receives one point. The points are added together for each alternative, with the highest scoring alternative being first in the social ranking, the second highest being second in the social ranking, and so on. Ties are counted as alternatives among which the society is indifferent. The Borda rule is responsive because it depends upon the individuals' preference rankings. Consider the full set of alternatives [x, y, z]. If we apply the Borda rule to these alternatives, we discover that $xIyIz$. Next, eliminate alternative y. If we apply the Borda rule to the remaining alternatives, we discover that zPx is the outcome. We have changed the ordering of x and z without changing their ranking by any individual, thereby violating condition (I). If we conclude that we cannot decide between the outcomes of wIz and xPz, then we cannot reach a decision, in violation of condition (U). Finally, note that if we consider alternative w to be no decision, and make this alternative the last choice of all three individuals (as in the first chapter), then w is the outcome due to the group's inability to make a decision. But this outcome violates condition (P) *and* the Borda rule.

Now let us briefly retrace our steps, using the typology of decision rules. For the relationship between x and z, we may derive three results. The first result, for the set $[x, y, z]$ is xIz. The second result, from the set $[x, z]$ is zPx. The third result, obtained by considering two choice sets $[x,y]$ and $[y,z]$ and applying transitivity to the result, is xPz. If the first two results are considered together, the Borda rule is nonprivileged with respect to itself. If the first and third or the second and third results are considered together, the Borda rule is nonprivileged with respect to transitivity. In any of these cases, conditions (U) and (I) will be violated. One cannot describe the conflicting outcomes as indifference, since indifference between x and z was the first result. If indifference was the outcome, then the Borda rule (in the second case) and transitivity (in the third case) would be overruled. Neither rule would be privileged or nonprivileged; as conclusion (4) has predicted, no rule is possible under these conditions.

The preceding analysis illustrates how the typology of rules, and conclusions (1) through (5), explain Arrow's proof and some of the subsequent literature on an axiomatic, rather than intuitive, basis. But this typology may be used for a second, more important purpose. If one classifies rules before combining them, one may predict the conditions that will be violated. One may thus weigh the advantages of violating certain conditions against the advantages of preserving other conditions in each case. This ability leads us to just one of the contributions of Arrow's work, that is, the realization that we do not judge the "reasonableness" of conditions *a priori*. We set up, or accept, conditions for decision making because we have some idea of what we are getting ourselves into; the "reasonableness" of conditions for decision making depends upon our reasons for making decisions. We cannot rationally make decisions upon conditions unless we know whether these conditions conform to our purposes. The typology of rules allows a first step in that direction, by predicting the conditions a given rule will violate. These predictions still raise some difficult questions, however, which must be considered in any given decision context. I will take up some of these questions later in this chapter.

In the next section, I wish to extend the preceding argument further, by describing how this classification of rules also applies to the Prisoners' dilemma and the problem of collective action. I will proceed in two steps. First, I will show how, for our purposes, these problems are actually variations on the Arrow problem. Second, I will show how one may predict the conditions that proposed solutions will violate, using the typology of decision rules.

THE PRISONERS' DILEMMA AND THE PROBLEM OF COLLECTIVE ACTION

The social sciences, like the physical sciences, tend to promote similar discoveries from different sources in a given era. This has certainly been the case with the Prisoners' dilemma and the problem of collective action. Unlike Arrow's Impossibility Theorem, which is primarily associated with the work of one individual,[7] these problems arose in several guises during the postwar era, under such names as "the problem of collective action, the prisoners' dilemma, the free-rider problem, and the condition of common fate, depending on the context (or discipline) in which it arises" (Barry and Hardin, 1982:19). I refer to this problem as the Prisoners' dilemma, or the problem of collective action, since Hardin (1971, 1982) has shown that all of these interpretations are variations on a single theme.

This theme concerns the conflict between individual rationality and the nonoptimal outcomes it promotes in collective action situations. Individual rationality mandates defection, or noncooperation, in these cases. As a result, all players defect rather than cooperate. Their actions eliminate an outcome (all cooperate) that is preferred by all persons to the outcome reached when all defect.

The conflict is best illustrated using two individuals facing two possible strategies: cooperate or defect. In the simplest problem, the two individuals choose strategies independently of each other. For individuals A and B, then, one of four outcomes will result: A and B both cooperate; A cooperates and B defects; A defects and B cooperates; and A and B both defect. A and B will choose their individual strategies based upon the option that yields the highest reward, given all possible actions by the other player. These rewards are defined in the matrix below for all players and outcomes. A's reward is featured first in the cell, and B's reward is featured second. If both players cooperate, both receive a reward of 1. If both players defect, both receive a reward of 0. The outcome "all cooperate" is therefore preferred to the outcome "all defect" by both players. (The fact that both players recognize that complete cooperation is preferable to complete defection is an important assumption for our later analysis.) However, if one player cooperates and the other defects, the cooperator receives a reward of -1 and the defector receives a reward of 2.

Player B

	cooperate	defect
cooperate	(1,1)	(-1,2)
defect	(2,-1)	(0,0)

Player A

Because of the reward structure, individual rationality directs each player to defect regardless of what the other player does. Consider A's strategy first. If B cooperates, A receives a reward of 1 if he cooperates and 2 if he defects; A will therefore defect. If B defects, A will receive a reward of -1 if he cooperates and 0 if he defects; once again, A will defect. Since these possibilities exhaust B's options, A will defect regardless of B's actions. Since B is guided by the same considerations and rewards, B will defect regardless of A's actions. Both players thus reach the outcome with a reward of 0, even though both would prefer the outcome where they both cooperate to a reward of 1 each. Communication is no solution to the problem as stated; even if one person knows the other's intention, defection is still the dominant strategy.

Let us concentrate first upon the two-person Prisoners' dilemma game, acknowledging that it is equivalent to a collective action problem for a two-person group. Clearly, the decision rule that determines the collective outcome here is unanimous choice; both players must agree to a given outcome, since there is no means to coerce an unwilling individual to cooperate. Let us label the four alternative outcomes in the Row/Column matrix, as shown below:

Column

	cooperate	defect
cooperate	y	z
defect	w	x

Row

Obviously, each individual would rank his preferred outcomes as shown below, based upon the size of each person's reward:

	Row	Column
first preference:	w	z
second preference:	y	y
third preference:	x	x
fourth preference:	z	w

Let us follow Arrow's conditions and apply the given choice rule (unanimity) to the pairs of choices in these rankings. Beginning with $[y,w]$, Row prefers w to y and Column prefers y to w; the outcome for this pair is wIy (by Arrow's Axiom I, which states either xRy or yRx must be true).[8] Considering pair $[x,w]$, Row prefers w to x and Column prefers x to w; the outcome is wIx. But group preferences must be transitive across preference or indifference according to condition (O). Hence, wIy and wIx imply xIy. Y is not preferred to x, despite the observation that all prefer y to x. A similar result may be obtained beginning with $[y,z]$ and $[w,z]$ as choices; once again, the outcome is xIy. By this logic, there is no reason to expect all members to cooperate, since the two individuals define a group that is indifferent between the outcomes of cooperation and noncooperation.

Note that all of Arrow's conditions are invoked to show the contradiction here. Conditions (D) and (U) do not allow any other decision outcome besides xIw and yIw under the unanimous decision rule; Arrow's Axiom I also mandates these results. Condition (I) licenses us to consider the choice pairs in whatever manner we choose. The transitivity rule of condition (O) allows us to combine individual choices. Finally, condition (P) is assumed when we argue that the result should be yPx, even though this result is contradicted by the outcome, xIy.

At this point, we must ask why we should feel bound by Arrow's conditions as we consider the Prisoners' dilemma. After all, there is no determinism that binds us to these conditions in collective decision making. However, the structure of the Prisoners' dilemma problem does imply these conditions.

First, we assume condition (P) if the outcome of "all cooperate" is preferred to the outcome of "all defect" because all persons prefer the former to the latter. If we negate this condition, we have no basis for expecting cooperation as an outcome. Second, we cannot reach outcome y (all cooperate) simply by eliminating outcomes w or z, in violation of condition (I). In the noncoercive Prisoners' dilemma game, we can reach outcomes w or z in which one person cooperates and the other does not, if we can reach outcome y in which all cooperate, since there is nothing to force the defector to pay. We cannot violate condition (I) in this way without running afoul of condition (P), since if we cannot reach w or z, we cannot reach y. We cannot declare w or z irrelevant because we cannot reach a decision using all four alternatives $[x,y,w,z]$. This strategy would state that the outcomes in four pairs was indeterminancy, and not indifference for choices $[x,w]$, $[w,y]$, $[z,x]$, and $[z,y]$, in violation of Arrow's Axiom I. But our conclusion concerning condition (I) implies that we must be able to rank *all* alternatives if we can rank *any* alternatives. Hence, condition (U) is also implied. Finally, we cannot eliminate Arrow's condition (D), since no person may coerce the other to cooperate while the dictator defects. Indeed, even if a dictator could exist, w or z would be the outcome, not y.

We now arrive at the most controversial question, however; how is the transitive rule involved in the Prisoners' dilemma? There is no point at which descriptions of the problem explicitly invoke transitivity. But these descriptions do implicitly invoke this condition. We make the transition between individual preferences and the group outcome when we ask what would happen if all people acted in this manner. Correctly interpreted, this question asks "What would be the group outcome if all persons ranked the possible alternatives in this manner?" There are only two responses to this question. The first response is to apply the unanimous decision rule to each individual's entire set of preference rankings. Little implies that this is a possible means of deciding between alternatives (Little, 1982:274). This procedure is quickly dismissed, however, since neither of the alternative rankings is unanimously approved. Hence, the result is group indifference between all alternatives, including "all cooperate" and "all defect." If we apply the unanimous rule to pairs of alternatives, we must find some means like transitivity for combining the paired results. We arrive at the conflict between an indecisive outcome, xIy (by the transitive rule), and a decisive outcome, yPx (by the Pareto condition). No action may be taken. If we assume that any decision at all is possible given the four alternatives, then the latter procedure must be used. The irony here is that some version of the question "What if all persons behaved in this manner?" must be asked if we wish to predict an outcome, since all rational persons must be expected to rank the alternative outcomes in the manner described.

A similar logic governs the problem of collective action for groups of more than two persons. Hardin provides the analytical framework for expanding the Prisoners' dilemma beyond two participants by suggesting the following:

Let us construct a game matrix in which the row entries will be payoffs for Individual, and the column entries will be per capita payoffs for Collective, where Collective will be the group less Individual. The payoffs will be calculated by the prescription for rational behavior: that is, the payoffs will be benefits less costs. (Hardin, 1971:473)

Let us combine this framework with Olson's description of a "latent group." According to Olson, the net advantage (A_1) that a person receives from collective action equals his share of the benefit (V_1) minus the cost of the collective good (C). Hence, $A_1 = V_1 - C$. As Olson points out, if C is less than V_1 for any individual, the group is privileged and should succeed. If C is greater than V_1 for all individuals, however, the group is latent and will not succeed (Olson, 1965:22–23).

In any group of size n, the possible combinations of individuals paying or not paying toward provision of the collective good equals 2^n (Hardin, 1971:476). In order to consider Hardin's analysis in the context of Arrow's proof, let us begin by invoking condition (I), and selecting a subset of outcomes from which the Individual and the Collective will choose. (Recall that we are licensed to do so because the choice procedure must work for all outcomes if it works for any outcomes.)

Assume that the group is latent, such that $C >$ than V_1 for all individuals. It will therefore be in the interest of no individual to pay the cost of providing the collective good entirely on his own. Assume next that the entire group consists of N individuals, divided into N_1 (the "Individual," consisting of one person) and N_2 (the "Collective," consisting of the rest of the group). Next, let us describe a set of possible outcomes. If all pay for the collective good, all will receive a positive benefit; label this outcome y as before. If none pay for the collective good, none receive any benefits at all; label this outcome x as before. All will prefer y to x, and Olson claims that his logic will apply under these conditions (Olson, 1965:2). Next, let us define alternative z; here, N_1 pays for supplying the good and the others do not pay. This is the worst possible case for the Individual, as his costs exceed the benefits he receives by the greatest amount possible under these circumstances (see Hardin, 1971:476, for an illustration of this point with ten-person games). Finally, let us define a *set* of outcomes, w; this set consists of all possible outcomes in which one of the individuals in N_2 pays, and no one else does. Since N_1 will clearly prefer any case where another individual pays for the cost of the collective good, so that he may reap the benefits without paying the cost, any of the alternatives in w would be preferable to y, x, or z. N_1's preference rankings are thus defined as:

$$\underline{N}_1$$

first preference:	$\underline{w}$
second preference:	$\underline{y}$
third preference:	$\underline{x}$
fourth preference:	$\underline{z}$

But how will the group N_2 rank this set of alternatives? Some group decision rule must be used to rank alternatives, and as noted above, in the absence of coercion that rule must be unanimity. First, all persons in N_2 will prefer y, in which all obtain benefits by paying, to x, where none obtain benefits by not paying. Second, all persons in N_2 will prefer an outcome in which another person pays the cost of the collective good and they do not; the only outcome that fits this description is z, in which N_1 pays the entire cost. Because the set of outcomes w implies that some person in N_2 pays for the good, N_2 will not unanimously approve any alternative in w, since the responsible person (who must pay) will always veto this choice. The quality N_2 will therefore prefer z and y to any alternative in w, but will be indifferent between x and w. This conclusion follows for two reasons. First, alternative z is preferred to y, and alternative y is preferred to x, by unanimous choice in N_2. In any instance in which one person pays and the others do not, however, the contributor will always prefer the alternative where no one pays, since he will be better off at that point. The defectors will always prefer the alternative where one person pays to the alternative where no one pays, since they are better off at the former point. Hence, the choice of x over any alternative in w, or the choice of any alternative in w over x, can never be unanimous within N_2. N_2 must be indifferent between x and w. The preference orderings for N_1 and N_2 are thus presented below:

	$\underline{N}_1$	$\underline{N}_2$
first preference:	$\underline{w}$	$\underline{z}$
second preference:	$\underline{y}$	$\underline{y}$
third preference:	$\underline{x}$	$\underline{x},\underline{w}$
fourth preference:	$\underline{z}$	

Because the choice must be unanimous, it is clear that zIy and zIx in N; but then, by transitivity, xIy in violation of condition (P). A similar logic applies if we begin with any alternative in w. Adding another vote for some w over x can never make the neutral choice unanimous for wPx, since the dissenting voter still exists in N_2. Similiarly, adding a vote for some w over x automatically excludes xPw as an outcome. Hence, xIw and yIw (from the unanimous rule), and xIy (from transitivity). We have derived the result predicted by the logic of collective action, since y cannot be reached, even though all prefer y to x.[9]

A similar logic therefore governs two-person and multi-person groups in collective action, under conditions described by Olson for latent groups. More importantly, however, the above proof illustrates how the Prisoners' dilemma and the problem of collective action may both be considered special cases of the Arrow problem. Unanimous rule (which is necessary to generate group preferences) and transitivity (which is necessary to combine group preferences) must coexist. The resulting conflict between these two rules prevents a decision from being reached among any of the alternative outcomes.

Let us now retrace the steps in this proof by using the typology of decision rules. Olson, Hardin, and Rappoport have all posited solutions to the Prisoners' dilemma and collective action problems. If these problems are, in fact, versions of the Arrow problem, then any solutions must violate some of the conditions Arrow posits (since his theorem permits no solutions). By classifying the decision rules according to my typology, and analyzing strategies for dealing with these problems according to this classification, then we can predict the conditions that particular solutions will violate.

The unanimous decision rule and transitivity must coexist in the Prisoners' dilemma problem. Because these rules are not the same decision rule (since unanimity is responsive and transitivity is doctrinaire), neither rule can be privileged. Hence, both rules are nonprivileged. If nonprivileged rules are allowed, any decision that is reached will violate conditions (I) and (U), and have the potential for violating condition (P). If we interpret the conflict between two separate rules as indifference, then we cannot reach a decision, in violation of condition (P), since such an interpretation negates the existence of *any* rules for decision making. The Prisoners' dilemma is merely a graphic illustration of this case; if we interpret the conflict between outcomes xIy and yPx as indifference between x and y, we violate the preferences of all participants. Indeed, this conflict provides the "sting" in the Prisoners' dilemma problem.

But what of the solutions posited by Olson, Hardin, and Rappoport? Olson states that a solution to the problem is possible if selective incentives are applied for contributors, or coercion is applied for noncontributors (Olson, 1965:132–34). Both solutions may be viewed as alternate sides of the same strategy: if contribution is made more attractive or defection less attractive by these methods, the chances that a rational person will contribute are increased. Rappoport has shown that this strategy works in a two-person Prisoners' dilemma game (Rappoport, 1982:78–79).[10] Let us assume in the classic Prisoners' dilemma game the reward for cooperation is increased by selective benefits, acknowledging that increasing the costs of defection by coercion will have the same effect. Consider the payoff matrix below, in which a selective benefit of three units is added for cooperators. Note that the labeling of alternatives remains the same as before.

		Column	
		cooperate	defect
Row	cooperate	y (4,4)	z (-1,3)
	defect	w (3,-1)	x (0,0)

Clearly, narrowly rational individuals would rank their preferences in the following manner:

	Row	Column
first preference:	y	y
second preference:	w	z
third preference:	x	x
fourth preference:	z	w

By applying the unanimous choice rule and transitivity to these preference rankings, the following results are obtained: xIw, xIz, yPx, yPw, and yPz. The outcomes for choices between x and y are consistent, whether we begin with the single pair $[x,y]$, or with any combination of pairs joined by the transitive rule. Two implications follow from this result. First, we have still not reached an outcome for the preference rankings in the classic Prisoners' dilemma problem; we have reached an outcome by rearranging those rankings. Second, we have not changed the orderings of y and x between the "workable" and "unworkable" preference orderings. Hence, we have violated conditions (U) and (I), respectively, as predicted using the typology of rules. The results will be the same for any n-person Prisoners' dilemma game, thereby extending this conclusion to the problem of collective action.[11]

Hardin solves a particular set of n-person Prisoners' dilemma games by a strategy similar to Olson's strategy (although his conclusions from this solution differ in important ways from Olson's conclusion). Hardin advises eliminating unrealizable outcomes and applying coercion to reinforce the resulting Condorcet choice of "all cooperate" (Hardin, 1971:477). Eliminating outcomes by choice or coercion violates condition (U) by acknowledging that no solution is possible if all alternatives are considered. Applying coercion to insure cooperation violates condition (I), since the rankings of "all cooperate" and "all defect" as outcomes have not changed from the insoluble configuration.

The "tit-for-tat" strategy described by Rappoport also proceeds in a similar manner (Rappoport, 1982:78). This strategy is easily described: cooperate on the first play of an ongoing Prisoners' dilemma game, and then do what your "opponent" did on the preceding turn thereafter. For instance, if I cooperate and my opponent defects, then I defect in the next game. If my opponent cooperates, then I cooperate in the next game. Under this strategy, coercion is introduced from outside a given Prisoners' dilemma situation—I cooperate in this instance because if I do not, you will punish me by noncooperation in the next. As Rappoport notes, however, cooperation cannot be encouraged in the last game under this strategy (assuming that players know which game is to be the last). By external coercion, alternative "y" becomes both players' first choices in all games but the last. Once again, the last game shows that we violate condition (U); similarly, we violate condition (I) by obtaining a different outcome in the last game than in previous games, even though the rankings of "all cooperate" and "all defect" do not change between games.

The significance of these conclusions goes beyond a mere illustration of the usefulness of the typology of rules; they also permit an evaluation of whether the authors' solutions to the Prisoners' dilemma problem affect the structure of Arrow's proof, which underlies this problem. On one level, Arrow's conclusions are not affected: one still cannot find a responsive decision rule that meets conditions (D), (P), (I), (U), and (O) simultaneously. On another level, however, Arrow's proof (or at least, the way we think about it) is affected. For we must ask whether the solutions posited by Olson, Hardin, and Rappoport are "reasonable," given the structure and implications of the Prisoners' dilemma problem. If we argue that they are reasonable—and I suspect that we would reach this conclusion—then we are in an awkward position regarding Arrow's five conditions. We state that (U) and (I) are reasonable conditions, but that the opposite of (U) and (I) are also reasonable conditions in certain decision-making contexts. Are we contradicting ourselves here? Note first that there is no logical contradiction. Conditions (P), (D), and (O), which are invoked in the Prisoners' dilemma problem, are compatible with the negation of conditions (U) and (I). I have proven this point before, since the former three conditions are compatible with nonprivileged rules, while the negation of (U) and (I) are a necessary prerequisite for the existence of such rules. But by noting that there is no logical contradiction in violating conditions (U) and (I), we admit that we had no logical reason, inherent in the other conditions, for accepting (U) and (I) in the first place.

Even if these solutions do not imply logical contradictions, though, is there not something highly unusual in finding an axiomatic condition reasonable in one context, while its negation is reasonable in another context? This result might be unexpected, but it is hardly unusual. In fact, a clear precedent for such a situation occurred in the development of non-Euclidean geometry. When Euclid set down the original principles of plane geometry, he began with five basic axioms. The first four axioms were intuitive; however, the fifth axiom did not derive from the others and was invoked as a "reasonable assumption" to explain the phenomena Euclid wished to describe. After Euclid, mathematicians attempted to prove the "necessity" of the fifth axiom by assuming its opposite and showing how this assumption yielded "unreasonable"— or more hopefully, illogical—results. These individuals wished to show that the negation of the fifth axiom was an unreasonable assumption. What these mathematicians derived instead, however, was non-Euclidean geometry, a system that explained another set of mathematical phenomena.[12] Olson, Hardin, and Rappoport have performed a somewhat similar feat with Arrow's proof. They negate two of Arrow's "reasonable assumptions" and obtain reasonable results for the problems they describe. Hence, the negation of Arrow's conditions may also prove reasonable in certain contexts.

It is useful here to recall a conclusion from a previous section: the "reasonableness" of conditions for decision making depend, in part, upon our reasons for making decisions. In the Prisoners' dilemma problem, we wish to reach the Pareto optimal point. One way of reaching this goal is to violate conditions (U) and (I) in the aforementioned ways. Are there other "reasonable" means of reaching collective goals, in violation of Arrow's conditions? The answer is limited by logic only insofar as we must avoid accepting contradictory conditions for decision making. Here, the typology of rules may be useful in exploring possibilities by helping to distinguish between impossible solutions involving logical contradictions and possible solutions that might, at first, seem to violate our sense of "reasonable" conditions.

Hardin appears to anticipate this critical distinction at the end of his seminal article on collective action. He correctly notes that "the threat of all against all [e.g. coercion] is not a logical necessity" for addressing the problem of collective action, but rather a "potentially useful device" to this end (Hardin, 1971:479). The preceding analysis supports this statement. Other possible ways of addressing this problem include: violating (U) and (I) in other "reasonable" ways; selecting a rule that is privileged and responsive, thereby violating the transitive condition in (O), while leaving the other conditions intact; and selecting a rule that is privileged and doctrinaire (and compatible with transitivity), thereby violating condition (D), while leaving the other conditions intact. These alternatives must be logical possibilities, if not practical or reasonable ones, since they preserve condition (P)—the condition that lies at the heart of the Prisoners' dilemma problem. These conclusions, however, raise questions about the relevance of Arrow's proof for decision-making procedures. If Arrow's conditions may be violated with "reasonable" results, we risk reducing his proof to the "mathematical curiosity" described by Dahl and Lindblom (Dahl and Lindblom, 1953:422); quoted in Barry and Hardin, 1982:231).

This judgment is premature and unjustified. Certainly, thirty years of scholarship on Arrow's proof is not based solely upon curiosity. But the above analysis does direct our attention momentarily away from the logical underpinnings of Arrow's proof. The problem is not that Arrow's conditions seem individually reasonable while being logically incompatible. The problem is that these conditions seem compatible to us. Hence, it is not of primary importance that the opposite of certain conditions may be reasonably compatible with the other conditions. We must determine why we (falsely) expect the original conditions to be compatible in the first place. Otherwise, we seriously reduce our chances for creating stable decision-making processes based upon preferences or opinions. If we do discover why these conditions appear compatible to us, however, we can derive clues to the "reasonable" manner in which we wish to violate certain of Arrow's conditions. In the next chapter, I argue that we understand the appearance of consistency between Arrow's conditions, and receive relief from the problem, by understanding the role of public opinion in public choice situations.

NOTES

1. Actually, Barry raises an important point here, even though he does not exploit this point to its fullest potential. Just because a decision has been reached,

that does not imply that this decision may be reducible to one privileged rule. This decision may be the outcome of two or more nonprivileged rules that do not happen to yield conflicting results in this instance. This is not to imply, however, that these rules would not conflict in another instance, and one should not consider the successful achievement of a decision as proof that it is based upon one privileged rule. A decision procedure that produces an outcome is *necessary* proof of a privileged rule, but it is not *sufficient* proof of one.

Barry goes on to make the point that one could establish indifference curves between two principles or rules that determine a decision, and that this would indicate that a decision was reducible to two or more principles. I perceive a problem with this conclusion, however; I would argue that the formula by which individuals balance the two principles is itself the privileged rule, and that the two principles are therefore not separate rules at all. This is not to say that Barry's notion of indifference curves and trade offs between principles is of no interest; indeed, I take up at length a related notion in chapter 5.

2. Unless, of course, the responsive rule requires only one person to decide the outcome; in this case, however, every single person could propose a different outcome, making the rule automatically nonprivileged with respect to itself. We are thus led back to the earlier conclusion that Arrovian dictators may not exist in a system governed by nonprivileged rules.

3. The nomenclature for these conditions, particularly the definition of the social welfare function as Condition O, are borrowed from Barry and Hardin, 1982:215–16.

4. Arrow's Axiom II states that if xRy and yRz, then xRz, where "xRy" means "the society prefers x to y or is indifferent between x and y" (Arrow, 1963:13).

5. Of course, one could argue, "but what if the rule states that some decisive subset—say a majority—rules, unless the decision is unanimous, in which case the majority does not rule?" Besides the fact that this is a rather bizarre case, it is also inoperable, as it is open to easy manipulation by group members; all it would require would be for one member to misrepresent his or her views, making the vote "less than unanimous" in theory, but actually unanimous in practice.

Similarly, one might state "but what if a doctrinaire rule states that it applies except in those cases where the group unanimously agrees to the outcome dictated by the rule?" One could argue that in this case, it is unlikely the doctrinaire rule would be invoked, but there is a response to this also—a dictator might take pleasure in being a dictator, and this pleasure might outweigh his desire for x to prevail over y. Hence, he might invoke the doctrinaire rule just for the pleasure of being contrary. As in the case above, however, this situation is also open to manipulation. If the dictator invokes the rule to create a situation of "not xPy," then the others need only change their votes to agree with him. The dictator will then change his choice again, so that xPy prevails, and all will be happy. As individuals who have served on committees know too well, sometimes the best way to deal with a pathology is to cater to it.

6. A more detailed version of this proof would run as follows. Let us begin with condition (P): if all prefer x to y $=>$ xPy. Let us also assume that one individual, i, prefers y to x while all others prefer x to y. There are three social choices that may exist given this preference configuration: xPy, yPx, or xIy.

1. If yPx, then i is a dictator. If a dictator exists, then a privileged and doctrinaire rule must exist. There can be no conflict of rules under this circumstance, and indifference will be defined only if the described rule includes an indifference point.

2. If xPy, then one of the rules being used is not doctrinaire (privileged or nonprivileged), since yPx could not block or overrule this outcome. Two possibilities remain.

   a. If the rule is privileged and responsive, then there is no conflict between rules, and the indifference point is defined by the described rule.

   b. If there are two or more nonprivileged rules that are responsive, then the rules must have different sized decisive subsets, and hence, different indifference points. As such, the rules will judge xIy at different points. If one rule (say A), produces indifference where another rule (say B) produces a different outcome, and if the conflict is defined as indifference, then rule A prevails. But rule A cannot prevail if both rules are nonprivileged. The rules may thus not be privileged or nonprivileged, so that the conflict may not be defined as resulting in societal indifference.

3. If xIy, then the rule is not privileged or doctrinaire, since i does not prevail. Four other possibilities remain.

   a. The rule may be privileged and responsive if the total group, minus one vote, is the indifference point. Here, there can be no conflict between rules.

   b. The rules may be nonprivileged and doctrinaire, so long as no rules have indifference points, or all rules' indifference points are the same. If these conditions hold, then the rules should be combined into one privileged rule, with conflicts being interpreted as indifference. If these conditions do not hold, then a violation similar to the one described in (2b) occurs.

   c. The rules cannot all be nonprivileged and responsive, for reasons similar to those in (2b).

   d. The rule(s) may not be a mixture of nonprivileged and doctrinaire and nonprivileged and responsive, for the latter must have indifference points where the former do not. Once again, the violation described in (2b) occurs.

Hence, if we begin with condition (P), then no conflict between two separate rules may be interpreted as indifference. Another way of stating this conclusion is that we must be able to decide between all alternatives if we may decide between any alternatives, since conflicts between separate rules negate the existence of any decision rules. If it happens that one of the alternatives is unanimously preferred to another under these conditions of conflict, then, (P) will be violated. Hence, there is always the potential to violate (P) under these conditions, and this potential will be realized if all possible sets of alternative rankings are considered.

7. Of course, the problem of cyclical group preferences was not Arrow's invention, but was actually discovered by the French mathematician, Condorcet, whose name is often associated with the problem.

8. Recall that xRy means "society prefers x to y, or society is indifferent between x and y," and that yRx means "society prefers y to x, or society is indifferent between y and x."

9. Indeed, one could do this proof more simply by considering the group

as a whole, with y being "all pay," x being "none pay," and w being "one person in N pays." Using the unanimous rule, it must always be the case that ylw and xlw under conditions of latency; hence, it is always true that xly by transitivity. I use the longer version of this proof in the text to illustrate the similarities between this problem, the Prisoners' dilemma, and Arrow's problem (the proof of which contains a similar division of the entire group V into decisive subsets and nondecisive subsets). Note, however, that in order to create the ordering in N_2, I had to apply the transitive rule to show z and y were preferred to x and w.

10. Barry has noted in a similar manner that it makes little difference in economic analysis whether one interprets this strategy as a reward for cooperators or as a punishment for defectors (see Barry, 1970:15).

11. Note that I have not considered Olson's solution that one person provide the collective good himself. The reason for this omission was described in the previous chapter, where I noted that if one individual provides the collective good, there is no "public issue"—or public decision—regarding this good. One could also interpret the provider of the collective good as a dictator, in violation of condition (D), since he or she provides the good regardless of the preferences of others.

12. See Richard Hofstadter's *Gödel, Escher, Bach: An Eternal Golden Braid* (1983), especially pages 90–92, for a fascinating account of these events in the development of mathematics.

4

The Spiral of Silence and the Rule of Privileged Choice

In the epilogue to *Rational Man and Irrational Society?*, Barry and Hardin analyze whether cyclical group preferences are correctly described as "paradoxical." The authors acknowledge the reader's discomfiture when confronted with the problem of cyclical preferences, explaining that one "may be inclined" to believe that if x is preferred to y by a group, and y is preferred to z, then x is preferred to z. They claim, however, that when we are confronted with the counterexample, and shown how z may be preferred to x even while all individual orderings are transitive, we "feel no inclination to hold onto our naive belief" about the group ordering (Barry and Hardin, 1982:376).

According to the authors, we easily abandon our belief when confronted with a counterexample. This is a logical negation (i.e. if cyclical majorities can exist $=>$ transitivity of group preferences is invalid). My typology of rules generates a more general logical negation: if both the responsive rule and transitivity are separate, privileged rules, then they may not exist simultaneously in all cases. But these responses are not complete, since our belief in the "reasonableness" of Arrow's conditions was not logically based. This conclusion follows from the case of the Prisoners' dilemma, where the conditions (U) and (I), and their negations, were both judged "reasonable" in different contexts. We cannot be expected to easily reject a belief to which we are inclined because of a logical argument or contradiction when that belief was not logically based in the first place. Yet, we must drop this belief. We therefore feel discomfort at this conclusion.

Our unease, however, leaves us with the decision of what to do next. Barry considers a similar problem of political evaluation in *Political Argument*:

> It may indeed be asked whether any argument is possible (let alone fruitful) concerning the ultimate bases for evaluation. If all arguments were deductive in form, there would indeed be no way of doing it, for in any deductive system there must be some axioms which cannot be proven within the system. But moral and political arguments . . . proceed upwards or downwards in generality. . . . It is therefore a legitimate and useful part of argument to show someone that a principle which he claims to espouse would have implications for certain concrete situations which he is unwilling to accept. (Barry, 1965:53–54)

We are working on the axiomatic level in judging between the responsive and transitive rules. Deductive logic will therefore be of limited use to us here. However, the converse of Barry's final statement suggests an inductive method for approaching the problem. He states that if principles lead to unacceptable conclusions, then these principles must be unacceptable when considered together. Conversely, if a set of principles is acceptable, then they must lead to acceptable conclusions. Herein lies the formidable problem posed by my preceding analysis: under what conditions may the combination of responsive and transitive rules appear intuitively acceptable, so that we derive acceptable conclusions from the result? This problem has two parts: under which conditions may this intuitive combination appear justified and do these conditions give a reasonable basis for choosing between the rules, or ignoring the logical contradiction? We cannot logically choose between the responsive and transitive rule; we can only conclude logically that we must choose between them. But we may not choose between them intuitively, since we began with the intuitive belief that both conditions should exist simultaneously. We are thus faced with a choice that we are ill prepared to make.

PREVIOUS RESPONSES TO THE PROBLEM

This problem has prompted two stock responses, neither of which is wholly satisfying for advocates of responsive decision procedures (and especially for advocates of democracy). The first response is that we expect the two rules to be compatible because they generally *are* compatible in the situations we encounter, and because individual judgments, if coherent, are responsive and transitive. If we have little or no experience with the contradiction on the group level, we are likely to carry over incorrectly analogous conditions from our individual-level decisions. The responsive rule and transitivity therefore coexist as nonprivileged rules. We violate conditions (U) and (I) with little awareness of the potential problems. Other authors have already reviewed several variations on this theme; I shall describe only two examples that illustrate this response.

A common version of this argument states that within a given group, individual preferences tend to be single peaked. The combination of such preferences is always responsive and transitive. This argument is stated in Duncan Black's analysis of committee decisions (Black, 1958:14–18), and Anthony Downs's analysis of political parties ranked on an ideological continuum (Downs, 1957:140). These solutions are limited, however, because single peakedness is a rather stringent assumption.

In another paper, I have argued that individuals' or parties' preferences in committees concerned with governmental budgeting could tend to combine into single-peaked preferences regarding budget allocations (Rusciano, 1984). This assumption follows because proposed expenditures are a standard indicator of priorities (measured in dollars allocated) and because the limitations on funds demand some coherence in allocating resources (and hence, in ranking these funding preferences). However, only one set of budgetary theories, not generally accepted by most students of the subject, assume such coherence (Rusciano, 1984).

Similarly, party preferences are often not as single peaked as we might expect, even in the most ideological contexts. In 1979, when West German voters were asked to rank their nation's three major parties in order of preference, they tended to be guided by their party allegiances and the accepted ideological classification of the parties. The results still came startingly close to being cyclical. If 7 percent of the voters changed their ranking of the parties, a cyclical result would have occurred.[1] If the results in both of these examples are unsure even under the best of conditions, the chances of single-peaked preferences under less stringent conditions are slim indeed.

Olson, Hardin, and Rappoport provide a second variation on this theme. They violate conditions (U) and (I) by using selective incentives or coercion to reorder preference rankings. Barry and Hardin argue that this solution is the one generally applied within democratic societies: "In real life true prisoners' dilemmas are rare. And because of this we tend to carry into our own thinking ideas about them that are relevant to other situations" (Barry and Hardin, 1982:385). Because these situations are rare, we do not experience the contradiction between the responsive and transitive rules. Yet, the authors undermine this conclusion by noting a clear weakness in Olson's theory of interest groups: the theory can explain contributions to an ongoing organization, but it cannot explain how the organization originally came to be created (Barry and Hardin, 1982).

This criticism must be extended to the iterated (or ongoing) Prisoners' dilemma situations that comprise our social and political lives—that is, how did these relationships come to be organized in the first place? In "Is Democracy Special?", Barry responds that many decisions in social life may involve single-peaked preferences (Barry and Hardin, 1982:338). This answer illustrates the common ground and the common limitations shared by these solutions.

To summarize this first response to our two original questions, we intuitively accept the combination of responsive and transitive rules because we lack experience with their contradiction. We ignore or discount the problem, at least as long as our luck holds out and we do not encounter it. But this is a rather insecure basis upon which to found responsive processes and institutions. As Arrow notes in the final sentence of Social Choice and Individual Values, "Collective rationality in the social choice mechanism is not . . . merely an illegitimate transfer from the individual to the society, but an important attribute of a genuinely democratic system capable of full adaptation to varying environments" (Arrow, 1963:120). Citizens of responsive systems may find themselves incapable of making decisions at some critical juncture due to this limitation.

The second stock response takes issue with the manner in which we define "responsive rules." Since Marx advanced the most systematic version of this argument, I shall concentrate upon it briefly here. Responsiveness, in the commonly accepted social choice definition, refers to individuals' perceptions or opinions of their interests (see Arrow's definitions of "welfare," 1963:25). These interests, as described by Olson and others, will be narrowly rational—and hence, economically based— in most public choice situations. But should "responsiveness" not then refer to individuals' true economic interests, rather than their perceptions or opinions of these economic interests, since these perceptions are often faulty? The common response is that individuals are the best judge of their own economic interests. Marx takes issue with this response; he states that most individuals fall victim to a "false consciousness" in defining their own economic interests. This false consciousness is imposed as a dominant ideology by a ruling class that benefits from individuals' false perceptions (Marx, 1977:516–22). Marx's evidence for these assertions is of particular interest, for his arguments depend upon an examination of Prisoners' dilemma problems that arise as individuals pursue their narrow interests in a capitalist system.

Marx's labor theory of value states that labor is the necessary element that creates value in a commodity—that is, the more "work-hours" it takes to produce a commodity, the more "value" that commodity contains. "Work-hours" are a standard measure, defined as the average number of hours of labor it takes to produce the commodity (Marx, 1975; Vol. 1:39). Any "average" measure, however, will be sensitive to the amount of variance individuals introduce into the total. An individual worker may produce more (and perhaps earn more) by "working harder," or producing more efficiently. In the former case, the worker produces more value by producing commodities at a higher rate than the average for all workers. In the latter case, the worker produces more value through the introduction of some process (organizational or mechanical) that allows him to produce commodities at a higher rate than average. The problem is that this single worker's productivity is then figured into the average that forms the basis for determining the value of the commodity. If only one worker produces more, the average is hardly affected; the worker comes out far ahead. If all workers produce more, however, the net result will be that all workers will be in a worse position than before; they work harder to produce the same amount of value (even though they produce a greater number of less valuable commodities).

The individual worker attempts to improve his lot by producing more; yet if all produce more, the result is the same wage for harder, more concentrated work. Hence, the worker is worse off than before. Marx's discussion of piecework illustrates this problem, although the argument will apply in any situation where workers receive rewards for greater individual productivity (Marx, 1975; Vol. 1:551–58). Marx argues that capitalists face a similar problem. Mechanization may improve the amount of average value a given capitalist temporarily receives; but other capitalists will quickly follow suit by adding similar machines of their own. The original capitalist's advantage is thus erased. The result, according to Marx, is a falling rate of profit for all capitalists, which eventually precipitates the demise of the system (Marx, 1975; Vol. 3:211–31).

The preceding analysis fits easily into the classic Prisoners' dilemma framework. It is in all workers' interests to agree to produce commodities at an acceptable set rate, so that their physical and mental powers are not overly taxed. The individual worker will be tempted to "defect" from this rate, however, in order to produce more than the average, earn more wages, and perhaps accumulate capital. If all workers behave in this manner, their defections will lower the average value of the commodity, leaving them with lower wages for more work. But the worker who "cooperates" by maintaining the old rate would be punished by losing his job, due to low productivity.[2] Hence, according to Marx, individual workers display a "false consciousness" concerning their true economic interests when they believe they can advance themselves by working harder. All workers "defect" from the slower average to improve their condition and end up in a position worse than if they had all "cooperated" to preserve the previous average.

The capitalist class also falls victim to this logic, since the falling rate of profit is another version of the Prisoners' dilemma problem. Certainly, all capitalists would be "better off" if they agreed to a set price for commodities and did not try to undercut each others' prices by introducing mechanization or other laborsaving methods. But the urge to "defect" and seize a larger market share is too great. Capitalists mechanize or lose out to those who have done so, and the rate of profit for commodities falls accordingly. Olson notes this problem when he describes why cartels are necessarily unstable and nearly always fail to set prices (Olson, 1965:40–51). Ironically, he recalls Marx's analysis, but fails to connect Marx's argument with the logic of collective action. Instead, he believes the two theories contradict each other and that his theory is more accurate. I will return to this point shortly.

Let us view Marx's version of the Prisoners' dilemma problem in terms of the typology of decision rules. Marx's problem, like any Prisoners' dilemma problem, rests upon a conflict between the transitive decision rule and the responsive rule. He attacks this problem by questioning the validity of the responsive rule's definition. The definition of a responsive rule (2a) requires that individual opinions or preferences be known before such a rule may be applied. From Marx's argument, the only justification for a responsive rule is that individuals are the best judge of their own interests. Such rules are actually meant to be responsive to individuals' interests, for which their opinions or preferences are the best indicator. Marx then argues that the Prisoners' dilemma inherent in the labor theory of value under capitalism "proves" that individual opinions about their "true" economic interests are faulty. He advances an alternative principle by which individuals' actual interests may be judged for social decisions. For communist society, this principle (stated simply) is "From each according to his ability, to each according to his need" (Marx, 1972:325).[3] He negates the definition of responsive rules based upon opinions or preferences, and replaces this definition (at least in the most advanced stages of communist society) with this principle. If one accepts this principle as valid and workable, then Marx's argument is also acceptable. For would it not make sense to use this principle, rather than individual opinions, to make responsive social decisions? Indeed, would these decisions not be more responsive than decisions based upon opinions or preferences, which are often imperfect reflections of individuals' "true" interests?

Here we must carefully distinguish between what Marx's theory does, and does not, accomplish. If we define "responsiveness" in this manner, then by definition Marx's proposal must solve the Prisoners' dilemma problem in the labor theory of value under capitalist production. A privileged rule that is responsive and doctrinaire (and that creates transitive social decisions, as Marx's principle does) may not meet all of Arrow's five conditions, but it satisfies the reasons justifying those conditions. Consider that Arrow's proof bars doctrinaire rules because such rules violate condition (D) by allowing the existence of a dictator—that is, a person who determines the social decision regardless of others' opinions. Once "others' opinions" become irrelevant for the application of a principle based upon individuals' "true" interests, however, the sting of dictatorship is removed. In this sense, Marx's image of the "dictatorship of the proletariat" goes beyond mere word play (Marx, 1972:331). It describes a system guided by the proletariat's "true" interests, not by "faulty" opinions or preferences about their interests.

This reasoning depends, of course, on the validity of Marx's equation of his principle with the "true" interests underlying workers' preferences. On this basis, we should note what Marx's theory does not accomplish. Marx does not describe a logical outcome of the Prisoners' dilemma problem in the labor theory of value under capitalist production. Recall the three possible solutions to the Prisoners' dilemma (and the Arrow problem) that I described in response to Hardin's critique of Olson's solution: demoting transitivity and the responsive rule to nonprivileged status, creating a rule that is privileged and doctrinaire, or creating a rule which is privileged and responsive. Olson opts for the first solution. His solution is thus possible and perhaps "reasonable" in certain contexts; it is not, as Hardin has noted, a logical outcome of the problem. Marx opts for the second solution. His solution is thus possible, and may be "reasonable" in certain contexts; but it is also not a logical outcome of the problem.

For this reason, Olson's critique of Marx fails to confront Marx's argument directly. Olson attempts to use his "logic of collective action" to refute what he calls the "logic of Marxian theory" (Olson, 1965:105). If Olson's solution to the Prisoners' dilemma problem were logical, then it would follow that the Marxist solution he critiques would necessarily be illogical; a logical solution, and its negation, may not be simultaneously true. But Olson's solution is not "logical"—it is "reasonable," given certain decision contexts. Hence, when Olson states that rational workers will not support class-oriented actions due to their perceived interests (Olson, 1965:105), Marxist theorists would reply that this only illustrates the inadequacy of workers' perceptions of their "true" interests. While the Marxist response may be "reasonable," it is also not a logical outgrowth of the Prisoners' dilemma problem. Indeed, when Olson or Marx claim a logical justification for their solutions, they become trapped in their own paradigms to the exclusion of other possible solutions (see Sabia, 1988:50–71, as an example of the Marxist response).

Is Marx's solution reasonable, however? Certainly, liberal thinkers would find his solution, or a state based upon Marxist principles (or any other privileged and doctrinaire rule) to be abhorrent. But this is merely to state the obvious. I prefer to judge Marx's response to my two original questions by the same criteria as I judged the first response—the consistency of the solution with the phenomena it describes. Let us summarize Marx's answers to my two questions. First, Marx argues that workers combine the two decision rules (i.e. responsive and transitive) in their relations with each other because their "false consciousness" leads them to believe they may thus advance their interests. Second, Marx argues that workers may only solve this problem by governing their economic and social relations according to principles based upon their "true" interests. Opinions or preferences are thus discounted for social decisions; instead, social decisions are made by application of a privileged and doctrinaire rule.

These conclusions assume the labor theory of value to be essentially complete. There are important questions about the place of opinions or preferences in this equation left unanswered, however. The labor theory of value states that if commodity X has value, then commodity X requires labor to produce. Labor is thus necessary for the creation of value. But is it sufficient? One could argue formally that it is sufficient, based upon Marx's theory. One may always calculate the average number of work hours needed to produce a given commodity and affix a "value" to it, but such calculations are somewhat artificial. If I produce a commodity that no one wants, am I really correct in affixing any value to it at all? Of course, this is to equate what Marx calls "value," with what he calls "use-value" and "exchange-value." Yet, if there is no necessary relationship between the two, then much of what Marx states about the price and value of labor also becomes invalid. Indeed, Marx asserts a version of this argument himself regarding commodities:

Their exchange . . . puts them in relation with each other as values, and realizes them as values. Hence commodities *must be realized as values before they can be realized as use-values.*[4]

On the other hand, they must show that they are use-values before they can be realized as values. For the labour spent upon them counts effectively only in so far as it is spent in a form that is useful for others. *Whether that labour is useful for others, and its product consequently capable of satisfying the wants of others, can only be proved through the act of exchange.*[5] (Marx, 1975, Vol. I:85)

If labor is not sufficient to produce value in a commodity, then what is missing? The classical economists would argue that the commodity must also be in demand.[6] But what defines demand? If the commodities are not absolutely necessary for subsistence, then demand is defined by preferences or opinions. This conclusion is particularly important for public choice analysis, which only deals with problems of allocation past the subsistence level. As Barry notes in the introduction to *Political Argument*: "it is only when the mass of the members of society have the possibility of living at something above the subsistence level that . . .

rather refined distributive questions . . . have very much application"
(Barry, 1965:xviii). If the labor theory of value must include preferences
in the calculation of value, then Marx errs in defining a system of decision
making based upon a privileged and doctrinaire rule. Indeed, Lindblom
makes a similar point when he notes how communist systems cannot
reach simple decisions regarding coordination of production and distribution because these decisions are not balanced through the supply and
demand of individual exchanges (Lindblom, 1978:101–102).

Marxists do have a response to this criticism: "true demands" can
only be known under a communist system, where "true needs" may
emerge. Capitalist systems generate "false demands" or "false needs"
to provide new markets for commodities and perpetuate the system.
Marx states this idea explicitly in *Die Grundrisse*:

As soon as consumption emerges from its initial state of natural crudity and
immediacy—and, if it remained at that stage, this would be because *production
itself had been arrested there*—it becomes itself mediated as a drive for the object.
The need which consumption feels for the object is created by the perception of it. The
object of art—like every other product—*creates* a public which is sensitive to art
and enjoys beauty. Production thus not only creates an object for the subject,
but also a subject for the object. (Marx, 1973:92; emphases mine)

With this argument, however, Marx's statements about production and
demand become tautological. Excess demand is necessary for capitalist
systems to exist, while capitalist systems must create excess demand in
order to survive. This argument raises the question of how "excess
demand," or capitalist systems, come into being in the first place.

A second problem with the establishment of a privileged and doctrinaire rule is that this solution is self-fulfilling. Marx claims that this rule
represents citizens' "true interests"; if these interests cannot be verified
(or refuted) by citizens' opinions, however, Marx's solution may not be
proven false. If we accept the ability of a system to reach a decision in
the Prisoners' dilemma problem (or to avoid that problem entirely) as
evidence of a doctrinaire rule's validity, then by definition Marx's doctrinaire rule is valid. But this is a rather weak measure of validity, for
any rule that is privileged and doctrinaire (and transitive) is by definition
valid. We thus have license to define the privileged rule in terms of
ethnic purity (as in Nazism) or divine revelation (as in fanatical theo-
cracy). The foundation of a privileged and doctrinaire rule makes all
such systems comparable, as in Lindblom's classifications of these systems as Model 1 types. Indeed, these systems do not exhaust the (often
heinous) forms that doctrinaire rules may define. All are valid using
criteria similar to Marx's criteria because all yield a solution to the Prisoners' dilemma problem whereby citizens are "better off"—albeit according to some prior definition of citizens' welfare and interests.

Of course, doctrinaire rules need not always conflict with citizens' opinions. In certain cultures or times these rules might prove quite popular. When the rule does conflict with opinions, however, it overrides opinions (recall the definition of a privileged rule)—hence, states founded upon such rules usually establish means to insure their decisions are followed. In this sense, Lenin's analysis grows logically out of Marx's analysis: a small cadre of disciplined party members is necessary and sufficient to administer a Marxist state. They are sufficient when opinions correspond to the doctrinaire description of citizens' "true" interests; they are necessary when citizens' opinions and the doctrinaire rule clash (Lenin, 1929). Whether this puts the sting back into Arrovian dictatorship depends upon one's faith in the doctrinaire rule as a definition of citizens' true interests.

It is this last feature of systems based upon privileged and doctrinaire rules that promotes anxiety among advocates of liberal systems, for if citizens depend only upon the first response to our questions (i.e. making the responsive and transitive rules nonprivileged) to handle the challenges of governance, they may find themselves unable to reach critical decisions. Systems based upon privileged and doctrinaire rules can always reach decisions. Hence, liberal systems seem less stable and more vulnerable than doctrinaire systems. If this were all one could say about the problem, Arrow's final warning would be justified. However, a third response to my two original questions uses the propositions from chapter 2 to show how democracy, as a responsive rule, may become privileged.

A THIRD RESPONSE

Let us begin again with the first of my original questions—under what circumstances may the intuitive combination of responsive and transitive rules be justified? The most obvious case occurs in individual decision making; an individual's decisions are always responsive if based upon his preferences, and transitive if coherent. Plott cites studies by Tversky (1969) and Lichtenstein and Slovic (1971) as evidence that intransitive individual preferences are rare (Plott, 1982:238). Many analysts thus attribute our intuitive combination of the responsive and transitive rules to a faulty analogy between individual and group preferences. Yet, this explanation is incomplete, for individual decisions are merely a subset of a genus of decisions that are always privileged and responsive—unanimous group choices. If a group of any size always makes unanimous choices (or even nearly unanimous choices in most cases), its decisions will conform to both rules, assuming as before that all individuals' choices are transitive.[7] Individual decisions conform to both rules as unanimous decisions for a group containing one person.

Of course, individual decisions might be the most interesting case in this genus, since unanimous decisions become rarer as group size increases. But what if it appeared that all responsive decisions were unanimous or nearly unanimous? Consider the effects of Proposition II from chapter 2:

Proposition II If an individual perceives he is in the minority on an issue, he is less likely to express his opinion. This tendency toward public silence will increase, as the number in the minority willing to express their opinions decreases, until the minority opinion is virtually silenced.

If the minority opinion is virtually silenced, then the majority opinion appears to be unanimous or nearly unanimous. Assuming that individual opinions are transitive, the observer would assume that these "unanimous" group decisions will always be transitive. If the majority opinion appears unanimous, then transitivity will appear to be a reasonable rule.

Consider now the case of cyclical majorities for the set $[x,y,z]$. If the majority chooses x over y and y over z, we might tend to expect that x is preferred to z by the above logic. Or would we? Here, we must invoke Proposition III from the previous chapter:

Proposition III Individuals tend to perceive when a position is gaining or losing strength in the population. Hence, the sum of individual opinions, and the sum of perceived majority opinions, tend to covary over time.

Because individuals tend to perceive the emergence of a majority opinion on an issue, they will only expect x to be preferred to z in the previous case if a majority prefers x to z. Since a majority prefers z to x, however, zPx will be the expected outcome. When faced with this dichotomous choice, the perception of majority opinion, and not the assumption of group transitivity, determines individuals' expectations.

Will individuals actually abandon the transitive rule when faced with an opposing majority opinion? They must if the perception of majority opinion as unanimous appeared to validate the transitive rule in the first place. If we perceive majority opinions as unanimous (or nearly unanimous), then transitivity appears valid. But if we perceive majority opinions as unanimous or (nearly unanimous), then x is not preferred to z in the above case, since a majority prefers z to x. Transitivity is overridden as a decision rule. The second and third propositions generate the expected validity of the transitive rule; these propositions thus also override this expectation when circumstances warrant. We abandon the transitive rule with little thought in our paired choices. This conclusion follows from Proposition I:

Proposition I In order for a preference to be considered in collective decision making, that preference must be communicated in some manner. As such, if any preference cannot be communicated, it may not become the social decision.

If a preference for z over x is the majority opinion, a preference for x over z will not tend to be communicated. The latter cannot become the social decision, despite our prior expectations.

These arguments recall my point regarding the different meanings of "public" in chapter 1: public opinion precedes public choice. Public opinion explains why the transitive rule seemed valid in public choice situations and why the transitive rule is invalid. We thus derive the second part to this "third response" to my two original questions regarding the combination of the responsive rule and transitivity. Public opinion allows us to reject the transitive rule, since that rule's validity was initially based upon perceptions promoted by the public opinion process. We negate the transitive rule whenever it conflicts with the responsive rule, making the responsive rule privileged.

This result may be derived from Arrow's proof, my typology of rules, and the above propositions. A privileged and doctrinaire rule is necessary and sufficient to allow a dictator; hence, condition (D) is necessary and sufficient to disallow such rules. The transitive rule in condition (O) allows for the existence of a dictator by establishing a privileged and doctrinaire rule. But a dictator is a person whose preference become the social preference regardless of others' preferences. By Proposition II, an individual's preference cannot even be communicated regardless of others' preferences. By Proposition I, if a choice cannot be communicated, then it cannot become the social choice. Hence, a person's preference may not become the social choice regardless of others' preferences. A dictator may not exist under these conditions. Similarly, one person's preference may also not block the social choice regardless of others' preferences. One must still dissent from a decision desired by others in order to block it—an option disallowed by Propositions I and II. Hence, neither a "nonprivileged dictator," nor a rule that is nonprivileged and doctrinaire, may exist.

Several questions remain, however. First, which responsive rule or rules will govern decisions? Second, will the rule(s) be privileged or nonprivileged? (We have only eliminated privileged and nonprivileged doctrinaire rules; rules might still be nonprivileged and responsive.) I will argue that the rule will be privileged and responsive, as a "third response" to my two questions. Further, the responsive rule will be democracy, or rule by the majority. For this to be the case, however, three qualifications must be met:

1. The rule must generate unique outcomes in every case, such that there are not two or more outcomes for a given set of preferences;
2. The responsive rule must be the best rule out of all possible choices; and
3. The responsive rule must eliminate all other possible decision systems that might be chosen.

If Qualification (1) is not met, the rule becomes nonprivileged with respect to itself and may not be privileged. If Qualification (2) is not met, then two possibilities arise. A superior rule may be chosen as the privileged rule, or some other rule(s) that are equally good may be chosen, making all rules nonprivileged. Qualification (3) follows from the Rule of Privileged Choice.

Majority rule meets the first qualification. Only one alternative may receive more than 50 percent of the vote; if no alternative receives more than half the vote; the society is indifferent between choices. However, any rule that requires more than 50 percent group approval will generate unique choices. The second and third qualifications must restrict our possibilities further if majority rule is to be privileged.

A particularly pernicious qualification is the third, which demands that a responsive and privileged rule eliminate all other alternatives. Unanimous choice meets the first and third qualifications. It generates unique decisions and eliminates all other possible decision rules; all persons must prefer to use it if it is chosen to make decisions. Indeed, Buchanan and Tullock argue that this rule is the best choice in *The Calculus of Consent* (1962).

But this rule does not meet Qualification (2). As Barry notes in "Is Democracy Special?," majority rule will always be the best choice for a majority of individuals, since it insures that a majority's wishes will be fulfilled more times than any other rule (Barry and Hardin, 1982:332). But this rule does not meet Qualification (3); it will always be opposed by people who fear being potential members of the minority. Of course, those persons may simply withhold approval of democracy until their basic rights are guaranteed. However, "rights" can be so individually relative that meeting the guarantees demanded by all persons could paralyze the system's ability to make decisions. At worst, an individual could decide to be bound only by those decisions that are in his interests and threaten to question the system's legitimacy when decisions go against him. The system may coerce the dissenter into obedience or punish him for disobedience, but then the system depends upon coercion to legitimize itself and eliminate alternative systems. Coercion also raises a technical problem. If a system may not be created initially without coercion, from where does coercion arise, and if coercion may be generated separate from the system to legitimize it, would that coercion not be capable of legitimizing many systems of decision making (including systems that are not as responsive as democracy)? If we attempt to guarantee all persons' "rights," we are back to unanimous rule in violation of Qualification (2).[8] But if we do not guarantee all persons' "rights" in all instances, we may not be able to eliminate all other possible decision systems as choices, in violation of Qualification (3). Within the limits of narrow rationality, the problem appears unsolvable.

But is it really so? The three propositions referenced above suggest a different conclusion, my third response to the two original questions regarding the combination of the responsive and transitive rules. If democracy is the first choice of a majority of citizens, then it will tend to silence all other possible decision rules by Propositions I and II. Proposition II states that minority opinions eventually tend to be silenced; Proposition I states that if an opinion may not be expressed, it may not become the social choice. It therefore follows that minority dissent to majority rule may also not become part of the social choice. Majority rule eliminates all other possible decision systems as a choice and becomes a privileged rule.

Let us consider the problem of guaranteed rights in this case. If a majority feels certain rights must be protected before it will accept democracy, these rights will be accepted. But majority rule will still be privileged, since it has legitimized its own restrictions. Rights that a minority demands as a condition for accepting majority rule, however—including the right to be excluded from majority rule when the decision goes against it—will tend to be silenced and will not delegitimize the system. This reasoning applies particularly to individual claims for immunity from democratically approved laws. Democracy, supported by Propositions I and II, meets the three qualifications for becoming a privileged and responsive rule. The moral power of the argument that "all others comply with the majority choice" under a democratic system promotes isolation among individuals who publicly dispute this argument. Dissension from the majority principle thereby tends to be silenced in a democratic society.

Will this reasoning apply in everyday decisions as it does on the systematic level? The Rule of Privileged Choice requires that it apply on both levels. If the fear of isolation operates when the decision system is first established, it must also work in practice, since the same silencing forces are at work. Individuals will adjust their behavior and their expressed opinions to the majority's wishes in order to avoid isolation (see Noelle-Neumann, 1984). Ascribing this much power to the "fear of isolation" is, of course, a very stringent assumption. I will examine this assumption, and its limits and implications, in the following chapters.

Yet, if one accepts this assumption on the systematic level, one must accept that it will have a similar effect in everyday decisions. Public opinion does not "stop at the doorstep" of public choice. It follows that we may apply my reasoning to collective action problems in democratic societies. If public opinion facilitates public choice and helps solve these problems, my argument will be supported (but not proven—recall that we cannot inductively prove an axiomatic assumption). This analysis will occupy the sixth and seventh chapters of this book.

A few final reflections are in order regarding this "third response" to the combination of the responsive and transitive rules. I will re-examine the paradoxical qualities of combining both rules in decisionmaking, for my response presents a new perspective on the notion of "paradox" in public choice.

DOXA AND PARADOX

In his book *Collective Action*, Russell Hardin argues that the problem of cyclical preferences is misnamed as the "Voter's Paradox":

An antinomy is a statement that is only true if it is false. The sense of paradox in the Voter's Paradox is obviously weaker than this. *There is nothing a priori illogical in the fact that the properties of an aggregation are not the properties of its constituents* . . . a Voter's Paradox is logical, possible, and perhaps even somewhat likely . . . calling it a paradox is an exercise in persuasive definition. That there can by cyclical majorities is structurally too obvious for consternation. (Hardin 1982:39, my emphases)

If this problem did arise from a faulty analogy between the properties of an aggregation and the properties of its constituents, then Hardin's argument would be complete. But this description is not complete; hence, neither is Hardin's argument. Barry and Hardin state that we are "inclined" to accept the combination of responsive and transitive rules. Here, Hardin refers to this inclination as a result of "persuasive definition." But why is this definition persuasive in the first place? Why do we expect the two rules will coexist, and why does this problem appear paradoxical? It is insufficient to say that the term is persuasive because it is a definition. We are not persuaded because a term is defined in a particular way; we accept a definition because we find it persuasive. I have already rejected the argument that we combine the two rules due to a faulty analogy between individual and group preferences. Does my "third response" to this question describe an "antinomy," then?

I have argued that the transitive rule appears valid based upon the definition of public opinion operationalized in the three propositions from chapter 2. If these propositions are valid, then transitivity also appears to be valid. However, if transitivity always appears to be valid, then the three propositions that support majority choices in all pairs must be invalid. Thus, transitivity can only appear to be valid if it is invalid. Whether or not this reasoning qualifies cyclical preferences or the Prisoners' dilemma as "antinomies" (which are only true if they are false) depends upon how much weight one attaches to appearances in one's analysis.

However, the notion of "paradox" implies that appearances matter a great deal. Consider Barry and Hardin's description of the term's etymological roots: "The word 'paradox' comes from the Greek *para* (beyond, contrary to) and *doxa* (opinion) and thus means etymologically, 'contrary to received opinion' " (Barry and Hardin, 1982:372). The authors then discuss whether the Arrow problem or the Prisoners' dilemma draw their "paradoxical" qualities from opinions regarding their assumptions: "Those who talk about the Arrow theorem or the prisoners' dilemma as paradoxical do not, however, appear to mean simply that they are contrary to common belief. Indeed, it would be difficult to maintain that there *is* any common belief in either matter" (Barry and Hardin, 1982:372). But surely there is more to this notion of "contrary to common belief" than the authors realize. First, we should define "common belief" in this matter not as opinions commonly held among a representative sample of the population, but rather as a belief held about the likely outcome of the Arrow problem or the Prisoners' dilemma by people confronted with either situation, for upon what is our intuitive combination of responsive and transitive rules based, if not the common belief in the "reasonableness" of this assumption? Our acceptance of both conditions is not logically based. Our shared intuition and our shared discomfort regarding the combination of these rules are evidence of our "common opinions" on the subject. The problems are "paradoxical" in this specific sense.

But there is a second, and more important, side to the paradoxical nature of these problems. Does a sense of paradox remain in the problems once we understand the beliefs or processes from which they are derived? Let us initially consider the first two responses to my question regarding the intuitive combination of both rules. The first response states that we assume both rules may coexist because of a faulty analogy between individual and group preferences, and our lack of experience with the rules' contradiction. According to this explanation, we characterize group preferences in an incorrect manner. Once we understand our mistake, the conflict between the character of "opinions held in common" (i.e. group preferences) and our intuition about these preferences disappears. The sense of "paradox"—the sense of belief "contrary to common opinion"—is removed by the explanation.

Similarly, the second response, outlined by Marx, argues that we assume both rules may coexist because of a false view of our own interests. We discover our error once our "true interests" are actualized and revealed by the application of a rule "genuinely responsive" to our interests instead of our misguided opinions. Once our opinions are "corrected" by the application of this rule, the conflict between the character of "opinions held in common" and our intuition about these preferences disappears. The sense of "paradox" is once again removed by the explanation.

If we consider the third response to my questions, however, we reach a different conclusion. Here, our belief that majority choices tended to be unanimous or nearly unanimous was an "illusion" that grew out of the spiral of silence process. Our belief that transitivity and a responsive rule could coexist was, in turn, based upon this illusion. When we more fully understand the actual process of public opinion, however, we understand why we first expected that the two rules could be combined, and why this expectation was false. The combination of the two rules *was contrary to common belief, or at least contrary to the process by which we share and develop common beliefs or opinions.* Unlike prior explanations, the "paradoxical" quality of the problem, the manner in which the two rules' combination contradicts the character of group preferences and shared opinions, is revealed by the problem's roots in the public opinion process.

All of this analysis depends upon the reasonableness of my preceding arguments concerning the social power of the "fear of isolation." We cannot assume that these arguments are reasonable, even if they are consistent, without evidence that points to the presence and power of this motivation. In the next three chapters I will examine this evidence. Chapter 5 generates a formal model of collective action that includes the fear of isolation as a motivation and chapter 6 examines some quantitative evidence of the power of this fear in motivating individuals toward collective goals. Chapter 7 examines some qualitative evidence of the effects of this fear on the structure of the Arrow problem in consumer behavior, the Prisoners' dilemma in social situations, and the creation of institutions for social and political decision making.

NOTES

1. The three major parties ranked in this study were the CDU/CSU (the Christian Democrats, or right-leaning party), the SPD (the Socialists, or left-leaning party), and the FDP (the Free Democratic Party, or the "middle-of-the-road" party). Not surprisingly, party preference guided the respondents first choice in the rankings: 95 percent of Socialists ranked the SPD first, 95 percent of Christian Democrats ranked the CDU/CSU first, and 78 percent of the Free

Democrats ranked the FDP first. The rank combinations went as follows (where ">" indicates "preferred to"):

Rank-Order Combinations	Percentage of Respondents
CDU/CSU > FDP > SPD	24
SPD > FDP > CDU/CSU	34
FDP > SPD > CDU/CSU	6
CDU/CSU > SPD > FDP	20
SPD > CDU/CSU > FDP	10
FDP > CDU/CSU > SPD	2

The resulting paired outcomes are a majority of respondents prefer the SPD to the CDU/CSU (SPD > CDU/CSU), a majority of respondents prefer the CDU/CSU to the FDP (CDU/CSU > FDP), and a majority of respondents prefer the SPD to the FDP (SPD > FDP) of the persons who answered the question. This result is transitive. However, if 7 percent of the respondents had shifted their votes so that the fifth preference ranking was favored by 3 percent instead of 10 percent of the respondents, and the sixth preference ranking was favored by 9 percent instead of 2 percent of the respondents, the result would have been different. In this case, a majority of respondents prefer the CDU/CSU to the SPD (CDU/CSU > SPD), a majority of respondents prefer the SPD to the FDP (SPD > FDP), and a majority of respondents prefer the FDP to the CDU/CSU (FDP > CDU/CSU) of the persons who answered the questions. Under the best of ideological conditions, then, preferences still come within 7 percent of being cyclical—a result that lessens expectations that preferences will tend to be single peaked under less clear or confined circumstances. (This data is drawn from *The Germans: Public Opinion Polls, 1967–1980*, edited by Noelle-Neumann; 1981:196).

2. Indeed, he will probably also be derided as "lazy" for producing at a rate slower than the "norm" for other workers.

3. This principle actually describes a late stage of communist society for Marx, in which the problems of "equal reward" have been erased by the acknowledgment that workers have unequal needs. As he states in "The Critique of the Gotha Program":

In a higher stage of communist society, after the enslaving subordination of the individual to the division of labour, and therewith also the antithesis between mental and physical labour, has vanished; after labour has become not only a means of life but life's prime want; after the productive forces have also increased with the all around development of the individual, and all the springs of cooperative wealth flow more abundantly—only then can the narrow horizon of bourgeois right be crossed in its entirety and society inscribe on its banners: From each according to his ability, to each according to his needs! (Marx, 1972:324–25)

4. Hence, labor is *necessary* for the creation of value in a commodity.

5. Hence, demand is *sufficient* for the creation of value in a commodity.

6. The above quotation suggests that Marx would agree.

7. Note that without this assumption, the problem becomes uninteresting, since we would not expect intransitive individual preferences to sum to transitive group preferences.

8. Barry describes the problem of not obeying laws that are not in one's interest to obey as a version of the Prisoners' dilemma problem. He is, of course, correct, since both problems involve a unanimous decision rule and persons who have the option of cooperating with, or defecting from, the group's decision. Indeed, this problem is inevitable in all cases in which we depend only on a person's narrowly defined interests to approve majority rule. The rational person will always conditionalize obedience to majority decisions (i.e. cooperation) with the caveat "but only when it is in my interests to do so." This caveat makes majority rule equivalent to unanimous rule, with the latter's described limitations.

5

The Fear of Isolation, Fashion, and Collective Behavior

"Too much is expected of rationality." (Barry and Hardin, in the epilogue to *Rational Man and Irrational Society?* 1982)

This statement concerning the Arrow problem and the problem of collective action presents an incentive and a challenge for continued analysis. The incentive lies in Barry and Hardin's admission that narrow rationality is inadequate for making collective choice possible in many cases. As stated in chapter 1, the notion of "public" in "public choice" is inadequate because it does not allow for a consistent definition of the realm in which collective decisions occur. The challenge concerns my proposed solution to these problems from chapters 2, 3, and 4—that public opinion makes public choice possible in societies by threatening nonconforming individuals with social isolation. But this argument might ultimately only remove the difficulty one step for if the problems of social choice arise because we expect too much of rationality, is it justifiable to transfer this burden to the fear of isolation? Or do we expect too much of this motivation also, when we credit it with the explanation and solution of these problems?

Several studies of the fear of isolation hold promise for my proposed solutions. But this promise is only partly fulfilled; the studies do not provide an adequate framework for applying the conclusions to broader social settings and issues. Holicki (1984) systematically reviews the literature on the fear of isolation in small group and laboratory settings. This fear did create consensus in most cases, making collective action possible. Such studies are of limited applicability to the problem at hand, however, for two reasons. First, these studies do not bear specifically upon the Arrow problem or the problem of collective action. Their conclusions have evocative implications for these problems, but they do not provide an adequate test for the solutions proposed in the preceding chapters. Second, the studies often prove a point most public choice theorists are willing to concede, that is, social pressures in small groups induce individuals to cooperate when we might expect otherwise, based upon narrow rationality. Indeed, Hardin notes how Olson's discussion of group size and collective action implicitly assumes small group actions succeed due to "political-sociological advantages" that large groups do not enjoy (Hardin, 1982:40).

The spiral of silence theory explains the success of collective action in small groups by describing the exact nature of these "advantages" in terms of the fear of isolation. This is no small achievement, but I wish to go further in the present analysis. I wish to argue that public opinion facilitates collective action and decision making in a similar manner on the societal level. Here, the theoretical framework has yet to be erected and justified.

In this chapter, I wish to derive a formal model that shows the relevance of the spiral of silence theory to economic and social relations on the societal level. I begin with a critique of Fred Hirsch's *Social Limits to Growth*, a work that explains the social processes underlying preference expression in consumer behavior. I trace these processes to the emergence of "fashions," and hence, to the spiral of silence theory. I then show that conformity to fashion is a form of collective behavior that is inexplicable within the boundaries of "narrow rationality," as commonly embraced by economic and social choice theorists. Because this behavior is relevant to economics, it is similarly relevant to public choice, which draws its inspiration and assumptions from economic theory. A full model of collective action thus includes conformity to fashion and the avoidance of isolation as motivations. I trace the effects of these motivations through Olson's, Hardin's, and Schelling's representations of the problem and present a formal model for conceptualizing the trade offs individuals make between their private utilities and the avoidance of isolation. The discussion culminates in hypotheses describing the conditions under which collective action should increase or decrease in a society or group. These hypotheses are subjected to quantitative and qualitative testing in chapters 6 and 7.

FEAR OF ISOLATION AND INDIVIDUAL PREFERENCES

The three previous chapters implicitly challenge the public choice assumption that individual preferences are the independent variable in

Figure 2
The dynamics of preference expression

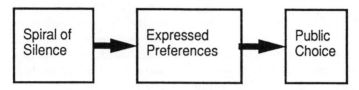

social decisions. Individual preferences must be expressed to be considered in social choice: hence, the preferences themselves are dependent upon a prior dynamic with important implications for the logic of collective decision making. Chapter 2 derived the propositions describing this dynamic from the spiral of silence theory. Chapters 3 and 4 explained how these propositions affected the "reasonableness" of Arrow's conditions and its related problems, the logic of collective action, and the difficulty of legitimizing democratic procedures. We now wish to develop a model that links the "fear of isolation" with individual interests in collective choice. This model must combine the dynamics of preference expression with the dynamics of choice, as outlined in Figure 2.[1]
In this model, expressed preferences become the intervening variable between the spiral of silence, which determines the opinions or preferences people may express publicly, and public choice, which aggregates these expressed preferences into a social decision.

This model must address three problems, all relating to the economic assumptions that underlie public choice theory. First, economic models tend to avoid discussion of the source of consumer choices. Although certain market research studies, which will be referenced later, show this reticence to be somewhat unjustified, we are advancing extraordinary assumptions for traditional economic theory. Second, even if certain economic theorists do consider the prior dynamics affecting consumer preferences, there is no guarantee that these processes can be related, or traced, to the spiral of silence theory. Third, even if the spiral of silence, and hence the fear of isolation, has a theoretical effect upon consumer choices, we may find ourselves unable to measure this effect with sufficient rigor to critique the public choice models. We are reminded of Barry and Hardin's admonition that "extra rational" motivations such as altruism, guilt, or fairness cannot be added into the collective action model without "credible measures of additional motivation." Without such measures, qualitative analyses of these motivations are probably more useful than the summing of "ill-defined units" of such factors (Barry and Hardin, 1982:52).

I advance three responses to these problems. First, I examine the work of an economist who deals explicitly with the sources of consumer choices—Fred Hirsch, in his *Social Limits to Growth* (1976). Second, I argue that a more complete understanding of the sources he describes leads one to the public opinion processes described by Noelle-Neumann's spiral of silence theory. Finally, I argue that the structure of Hirsch's analysis allows it to be combined with Noelle-Neumann's analysis (which in turn, allows us to create rough quantitative measures of the effects of the threat of isolation). We may therefore generate credible measures of the "value" of avoiding isolation, as manifested in consumer choices directed toward this end.

Hirsch begins his book at the departure point for public choice analysis, the satisfaction of subsistence needs: "As demands for purely private goods are increasingly satisfied, demands for goods and facilities with a purely public (social) character become increasingly active" (Hirsch, 1976:4). This distinction between public and private "values" of goods is central to a complete understanding of the "composition of consumption," which makes expressed preferences an intervening variable between actual demands and consumer behavior in the market (Hirsch, 1976:16, 146). The "actual demands" of consumers are often prompted by what Hirsch calls "positional competition" (Hirsch 1976:105). This competition determines an object's public or "social" value.[2] The competition occurs as individuals demand goods because of the status attached to those goods, or because of the absence of physical or social crowding that renders the goods less valuable, or even useless (Hirsch, 1976:21).

But how does one judge such factors as "status" or "crowding"? Hirsch admits, for instance, that the status of an object or an activity may be a function of fashion:

The social limitation may be derived, most directly and most familiarly, from psychological motives of various kinds, notably *envy, emulation, or pride*. Satisfaction may be derived from relative position alone, of being in front, or from others being behind. Command over particular goods and facilities in particular times and conditions becomes an indicator of such precedence in *the emergence of a status symbol. Where the sole or main source of satisfaction derives from the symbol rather than the substance*, this can be regarded as pure social scarcity. . . .

But the scarcity itself need not be associated with absolute physical limitations. It can be socially rather than physically defined, *through the influence of fashion*. Thus, a cachet of this kind can be attached, at a given time, to particular antiques which cannot be replicated, but derive their scarcity *value* only from the (changeable) fashion that designates them as a sought after item. Antiques in the sense of uncommon junk, and addresses of wavering fashion, are the main examples. Scarcity is, so to say, deliberately created and manipulated. (Hirsch, 1976:20–21; emphasis mine)

Once Hirsch opens the door by admitting that fashion may cause or determine "status" (and hence, value) in positional competition, however, he finds it very difficult to shut it again, for such "psychological" motivations as "envy, emulation, and pride" have a decidedly social aspect; others must desire or respect the object of such emotions before we perceive the object as satisfying these motivations. Noelle-Neumann recalls Hume's "love of fame" as the brighter side of the fear of isolation with reference to such emotions (Noelle-Neumann, 1984:75–76). Put another way, my capacity to "be in front" in terms of status derives primarily from the willingness of others to fall in behind my lead. All status is therefore a function of fashion, which becomes the critical factor in this form of positional competition (albeit with the caveat that certain fashions endure longer in a given society than others).

The concept of physical or social "crowding," which forms the second type of positional competition, encounters a similar definitional problem. "Crowding" is an individually relative term. A city that is hopelessly (and uselessly) crowded to a Vermont farmer might be relatively quiet and free of traffic to a native of Manhattan. The Ivy League degree that leads to a middle-level management position might be evidence of "social crowding" to an executive's offspring, who expected much more from this type of certification. But the same position might be a promise fulfilled to a laborer's offspring. The author avoids the individual relativity of this term with his metaphor of space, which links social or physical "crowding" to "positional competition." According to Hirsch, we desire a certain position relative to others in the society and make "defensive expenditures" to reach and protect this position:

Defensive goods . . . are a facet of some wants being a means of satisfaction of other wants. . . . The admission is a crucial one and serves to reopen an old philosophical problem of the purpose of economic activity . . . (there exists a) distinction between what consumers really want and what they do to get it. This distinction rests on an implicit two-fold division in consumer preferences. *The implied division is between goods and services that yield direct primary satisfaction in themselves and those that yield zero or negative satisfaction.* (Hirsch, 1976:59; emphases mine)

"What consumers really want" is to "protect the position of the individual (i.e. themselves) in the social environment" (Hirsch 1976:64). This desire defines the social or public aspect of expenditures mentioned above, but its satisfaction yields "zero or negative satisfaction." One derives utility from these expenditures through the maintenance of one's position. These expenditures allow consumers to avoid a "social bad" (Hirsch's term)—that is, to avoid incurring some punishment or penalty, to stay even, as it were. These expenditures "derive their value only from the negative factor being countered" (Hirsch, 1976:57).

Hirsch is somewhat unclear about the exact nature of the "penalty" consumers avoid through defensive expenditures. We may describe this penalty, however, by tracing "positional competition" back to its roots in fashion. If maintenance of one's status is the end in positional competition, then this penalty is avoided by conforming to fashion. I will argue further that avoiding the penalty in physical or social crowding also requires conformity to fashion.

Hirsch assumes that "crowding" is socially defined, in part because defensive expenditures directed at avoiding crowding are socially defined. But from where does this definition arise? The author avoids the problem of the individual relativity of crowding with a socially defined sense of the term: social or physical crowding occurs when it is generally perceived that an object has lost its value because too many people possess or enjoy it. But this argument only removes the question one step. From where does this "general perception" arise? The author answers that it originates with the society's elites: "The presumption that what the elite have today the mass will demand—and acquire—tomorrow has become deeply entrenched in Western society. It is the basic underlay for much social planning" (Hirsch 1976:168).

Elites define the desirable objects in the society; however, once the public acquires those objects, the objects lose their value in positional competition. Elites then desire (and obtain) other objects, which the mass then also acquires in a futile quest for the trappings of "elite position." This position must always elude the mass by definition, however, since the value of the position is defined by the fact that only a few people occupy it.

A problem arises with this analysis, though. The only proof we have of this underlying dynamic is that the public often desires what elites possess. Certainly, elites influence public tastes in many instances, but their possession of an object is neither necessary nor sufficient to promote public demand for it. The public desires many things that social elites do not possess and would find tasteless. Social elites possess many things that the public does not desire. But "defensive expenditures" need not be prompted by the possessions or actions of elites. When elites possess something that the rest of society comes to demand, they have affected the society's perception of what is fashionable to possess.[3] This conclusion suggests that *fashion*, and not the tastes of elites, is the proper subject for an inquiry into defensive expenditures.

Herein lies the transition from Hirsch's analysis to Noelle-Neumann's theory of public opinion. Fashion, which underlies Hirsch's notion of positional competition, gains its influence by threatening nonconformists with a social penalty (or a "social bad," to use Hirsch's term)— isolation. Fashion is a form of public opinion that coerces by threatening the individual with social isolation. Hirsch contributes to our understanding of this penalty by noting that this threat may prompt defensive expenditures aimed at avoiding the social penalty, and that these expenditures have been neglected in traditional economic analyses. Noelle-Neumann's examination of market research studies similarly reflects the critical influence of the threat of isolation on consumer choices:

It is always touching to read in market analyses how wistfully consumers answer the question of *what, above all*, they are looking for when they buy a new dress: "It should not go out of style." Here, if anywhere, we witness a genuine resentment against the "coercion to consume," an anger at having to compromise one's own inclinations to the demands of fashion in order not to be ridiculed or rejected by contemporary tastes. . . . But the reasons for this "coercion to consume" are misjudged. It is not storekeepers who pull the strings of these processes, as angry consumers tend to believe. They don't set the stage, steering the trend of fashion in one direction or the other. If they are successful, it is because like good sailors they know how to trim their sails to the wind. The outward garment is too good a medium for the individual to exhibit his obedience to society. (Noelle-Neumann, 1984:117–18)

In Hirsch's terms, the "defensive expenditure" in the above example is the purchase of a new dress; the "actual desire" is the wish to avoid isolation through conformity to public opinion. Hirsch advances our understanding of economic processes by assigning the avoidance of isolation an individual value or utility. Yet, he stops short of concluding that we may measure this utility with sufficient rigor to use it in economic or social calculations:

The relevant problem is not how much is the individual willing to spend on that activity or this purchase, but what for? The latter question cannot be answered in the precise and objective form of a sum of money and has thus far proved impervious to alternative quantification. For the purpose of economic measurement, then, the question remains nonoperational. (Hirsch, 1976:59)

If individual expenditures were the only indicator of the threat of isolation, then Hirsch's reticence would be justified. Similarly, if private utility and the social utility of avoiding isolation always pointed to the same behavior, then attempts at quantification would also be seriously hindered. But this is not the case for the Arrow problem and the logic of collective action. In the problem of collective action, the individual's private interest lies in defection, noncooperation, and nonpayment. We may also measure when fashion, or public opinion, directs the individual in the opposite direction toward cooperation. The climate of opinion and the individual's perception of the climate of opinion are powerful indicators of the path an individual must take to satisfy his "social" utility to avoid isolation. Hence, when the individual's "private" and "social" utilities conflict, we may measure the value or utility he assigns to avoiding isolation by the private gain the individual foregoes in order to reach this end.

This idea is analogous to the idea behind the Asch experiment. Defection is the "correct" response to fulfill an individual's private or narrowly rational interests in collective action, just as the matching line is the "correct" response in the Asch experiment. If individuals choose the "incorrect" response (i.e. cooperation) because it is the general opinion in the former case, then they are willing to exchange the profit they would gain from noncooperation for the avoidance of isolation. We achieve at least a rough measure of the former value or utility by this means.

This analysis assumes, of course, that the individual cooperates because the climate of opinion favors cooperation or because he perceives that it favors cooperation. But these factors are easily built into an alternative model of collective action, which may then be tested empirically. I will devote the next section to deriving this alternative model. I wish to conclude my discussion, however, with a statement in which Hirsch anticipates my further analysis. Hirsch does not specifically reference "public opinion" in this statement; yet, he implies the importance of the process by describing the prior neglect of "social conventions" by economists:

> In more casual friendship and everyday social relations, the public good of the norm of sociability will be crucial, dominating the direct benefit of private good aspect of the particular relations. . . .
> This is a peripheral example of an important social phenomenon: the existence of felt obligations to act in mutually supportive ways in given circumstances, formally undefined but grounded in the *prevailing convention of good social behavior*. Such obligations are usually considered the province of sociologists, and are regarded by economists as fixtures; which in practice means they are ignored. But social norms of this kind have a definite economic content, as public goods. For economists to exclude them from the set of interactions they are concerned with is to impart a bias in economic calculation [and hence, in public choice analysis] comparable to the bias in economic calculation resulting from the earlier exclusion of the economic effects of pollution or congestion. (Hirsch, 1976:78–79; emphases mine)

Similarly, we can ill afford to exclude the coercive effects of public opinion upon behavior in public choice analysis. The problem is to build these effects into a model of collective behavior that displays a rigor comparable to the collective choice model.

THE VALUE OF AVOIDING ISOLATION

Barry describes the confusion which arises in economic analysis when one excludes considerations of "social utility" from individual motivations:

One can be presented with people . . . who are "slaves" to custom, fashion, or the opinions of those with whom they associate. Galbraith's attack on "synthetic" wants and Riesman's obvious preference for the "autonomous" man rather than the "inner-directed," "other-directed," or custom-bound type are recent examples of writers who have been driven to adopt self-determination as a criterion in order to make decisions. . . .

An interesting complication is that Galbraith tries to force his case into a want-regarding framework and thus has to say that the satisfaction of "synthetic" wants should be ignored in the calculation of welfare economists. *Since however "synthetic" wants certainly are wants this is surely confusing.* (Barry, 1965:140; emphases mine)

Any description of the "value" or "utility" of avoiding isolation must be set within the context of a theory or model of "pure social utility," as implied by Hirsch's work. It is doubtful, of course, that anything approaching "pure social utility" actually exists. But this construct is useful for describing the interaction of individual and collective behavior in the creation of fashion—and more generally, public opinion—based upon the costs and benefits accrued by individual actors. More importantly, when one examines the problem of fashion, one finds it is doubtful that anything approaching "pure private utility" exists beyond the subsistence level, despite the assumptions of many economists. But here we are treading upon nontraditional and uncharted territory for most economic analyses, which deal almost exclusively with the private utility individuals derive from such exchanges. I justify this endeavor first by negation, for conformity to fashion though "defensive expenditures" cannot be explained in terms of pure private utility or the narrow rationality of the collective action model. But such conformity is a pervasive form of collective behavior in the marketplace and other areas of social relations. We therefore may either declare this behavior irrelevant to economic analysis or admit that individuals often conform to fashion to serve a social utility that outweighs their private utility. We know that the "fear of isolation" exists in individuals; we must prove that individuals will incur costs to avoid isolation.

Changes in fashion are a form of collective behavior. The Collective (to use Professor Hardin's term) determines what is fashionable for the individual. In practice, we consign last year's designs in neckties and shirts to the back of our closets because "no one wears that style any more." Our judgment of others' tastes, obtained and reinforced by our observation of the social environment, determines the fashionable expenditures we make and the fashionable actions we take. Let us assign to this expenditure (or this action) a cost of C.

In accordance with the logic of collective action, the Collective may have no motivations other than the sum of the motivations of its individual members. These individuals are motivated by narrow rationality or the private utility they derive from interactions with others. We exclude all notions of "social utility" from our calculations to remain within the strict boundaries of the collective action model. An expenditure made to "remain fashionable" (or to "maintain one's position in the social environment", to use Hirsch's terminology) has a cost of C. There is no monetary return from conforming to fashion. Hence the benefits of this behavior are described by the following matrix:

Collective

		buy	not buy
	buy	(-C̲,-C̲)4	(-C̲,0)
Individual			
	not buy	(0,-C̲)	(0,0)

The Individual's dominant strategy in this case of collective behavior is clear. The Individual should not buy, regardless of the Collective's actions. Since each person must be expected to reach the same conclusion (recall the analogous case with other forms of collective action), no one will buy. Hence, we must conclude that fashions do not change.

Clearly, this is an absurd conclusion. Fashions do change, often with disconcerting speed. Yet, we reach this absurd conclusion if we remain strictly within the boundaries of the logic of collective action. For if fashions do change, then by definition all individuals must generally conform to this change. We find ourselves in the upper left-hand cell of the matrix, contrary to our predictions based upon private utility. Our model of individual and collective behavior is therefore incomplete in this instance.

Should we exclude fashionable expenditures from economic analysis, then? We may term this behavior "irrational," but it is hardly irrelevant for understanding collective action. The gap in collective action analysis lies not in the theory itself but in the economic assumptions that underlie this theory. Fashion and public opinion are an ever-present force in the market, as in all other forms of collective behavior. Defining conformity to public opinion as "irrational" does not alleviate the bias in economic or social models that seek to exclude it.

But how may a model of "pure social utility" address this bias in traditional economic models? Let us assume that a social utility from avoiding isolation exists, and that individuals make trade offs between their social and private utilities in conforming to fashion. If we define the "social utility" of conforming to fashion as C', and if the individual is willing to pay C in order to reach this end, we may conclude that for the individual, $C' > C$, and the $C' - C > O$. In Olson's equation from the logic of collective action, an individual's net benefit equals the individual's total benefit minus the cost incurred in securing that benefit. From this formula, we may derive the costs and benefits that the Individual incurs through conformity or nonconformity with the Collective's fashion tastes:

1. If the Collective's tastes in fashion change, and the Individual conforms to this decision, both receive a reward of $C' - C$ (that is, the "social utility" minus the cost of the item). This follows because the Collective defines what is fashionable, and hence, behavior that conforms to the Collective's behavior is rewarded with the benefit of avoiding isolation, C'.
2. If the Collective's tastes in fashion do not change, and the Individual conforms to this decision, both receive a reward of C' (since no costs were incurred).
3. If the Collective's tastes in fashion change and the Individual *does not* conform to this decision, the Collective receives a reward of $C' - C$ and the Individual receives a reward of O.
4. If the Collective's tastes in fashion do not change, and the Individual *does not* conform to this decision, the Collective receives a reward of C' and the Individual receives a reward of $-C$.

Adding in the "social utility" of avoiding isolation by conforming to fashion changes our calculations of the Individual's dominant strategy. This result is evident from the payoff matrix for Individual and Collective behavior with "social utility" included:

Collective

		buy	not buy
	buy	$(\underline{C'} - \underline{C}, \underline{C'} - \underline{C})$	$(-\underline{C}, \underline{C'})$
Individual			
	not buy	$(0, \underline{C'} - \underline{C})$	$(\underline{C'}, \underline{C'})$

The Individual's strategy has become more complex. He should buy when the Collective buys (since $C' - C > 0$) and not buy when the Collective does not buy. If the Collective's tastes in fashion change, the

Individual's tastes must also change, according to this model of "pure
social utility."

I perceive three principle objections to this analysis, however. The
first objection concerns the logic behind the kind of exchange we are
describing. Will individuals exchange a tangible value (i.e. money) for
a somewhat intangible reward (i.e. avoiding isolation)? Can we define
such behavior as "rational" in any economic sense of the term? Downs
argues that we cannot in a passage typical of the response given by most
social choice theorists:

. . . even though we cannot decide whether a decision-maker's ends are rational,
we must know what they are before we can decide which behavior is rational
for him. Furthermore, in designating those ends, we must avoid the tautological
conclusion that every man's behavior is rational because 1) it is aimed at some
end; and 2) its returns must have outweighed its costs in his eyes or he would
not have undertaken it.

To escape this pitfall, we focus our attention only upon the economic and
political goals of each individual or group in our model. Admittedly, separation
of these goals from many others which men pursue is quite arbitrary. . . . Nevertheless, this is a study of economic and political rationality, not psychology.
(Downs, 1957:6–7)

Before we respond to this argument, let us clarify the exact nature of
Downs's complaint. The problem is not whether the goal of avoiding
isolation is "rational" for the individual conforming to fashion; as Downs
notes, goals or ends are never judged rational or irrational in economic
analyses. One may only judge the rationality of means used by individuals seeking to fulfill particular ends. The relevant question is thus
whether a discussion of "fashion," public opinion, and the fear of isolation properly belongs in the analysis of economic behavior. This question may only be answered by assessing the usefulness of including
these motivations in economic analysis, or the problems of omitting
them. We have shown that these motivations deserve consideration in
our model. Since "positional competition" and Hirsch's analysis are
useful conceptual tools, the influence of fashion and public opinion are
necessary components of our model. Similarly, the influence of fashion
is pervasive in the marketplace; thus, we must consider this influence
if we are to understand economic behavior more completely. To describe
avoiding isolation as an "irrational motivation" misses the mark.

It follows, then, that a model of collective action that does not include
the influence of fashion must be as incomplete as the models of economic
behavior that commit a similar omission. If the ends of collective behavior
are partially defined outside of the narrow cost/benefit analysis of the
collective action model, then the rationality of individual actions must
also be judged with reference to these additional motivations. The prior

dynamic of public opinion, which defines fashionable behavior and expenditures, must be included in the calculation.

The next two objections address this point more directly, for as I stated at the outset, it is doubtful that anything approaching "pure social utility" actually exists, for two reasons. First, our model still cannot explain *why* fashions change, even if the Individual follows the lead of the Collective. For the Collective (if I may refer to the other group members as a unit for a moment) still has "not buy" as its dominant strategy in this case. The Collective's reward is always higher if it does not buy, regardless of the Individual's actions (since $C' > C' - C$, and the Collective defines the location of C'). The second objection merely restates that the Collective may have no motivations or actions apart from the motivations and actions of the individuals who comprise it. To refer to the Collective as a single entity is unacceptable.

But both of these objections lead us to a useful conclusion for the model we wish to derive: there can be no discussion of "pure social utility" independent of a discussion of the private utilities of the individuals involved, beyond the mere subsistence level. This conclusion is the converse of the conclusion that we reached with reference to fashion—that is, there may be no discussion of "pure private utility" independent of the discussion of social utility in collective behavior, beyond mere subsistence. At this level, goods or actions contain both private and social utilities. A complete model of collective behavior must include both values. From this conclusion we may turn to a more complete discussion of collective action.

PRIVATE AND SOCIAL UTILITY

Before discussing the interaction of individual and collective behavior described above in Olson's and Hardin's terms, we must deal with an operational problem concerning "fashionable" expenditures. We have noted that "the Collective" determines which behavior is fashionable at any given time. Within a two-dimensional matrix that includes only the Individual and the Collective, this statement is sufficient to analyze collective action. But Hardin goes beyond this two-part matrix to more complex interactions when he discusses collective action (Hardin, 1982), and we wish to do the same. We are, therefore, faced with a problem: what number or proportion of individuals in a given group must embrace a particular behavior, or endorse a particular expenditure or action, before these decisions may be judged "fashionable" (and thereby, coercive toward the rest of the population)? At what point do individual preferences or opinions define fashion? Noelle-Neumann responds: "The threat of isolation is present whenever individual judgments manage to become prevailing opinion" (Noelle-Neumann, 1984:119). An opinion or behavior prevails when individuals generally perceive that "most people" (i.e. a clear majority of the population) embrace it (Noelle-Neumann, 1984:43).

Clearly, in most real-life situations, several factors affect an individual's perception of the majority position on a given issue. Hence, the actual climate of opinion (i.e. the numerical majority) and individuals' perceptions of the climate of opinion (i.e. their perceptions of what "most people" think on a given issue) are both important variables in our analysis (Noelle-Neumann, 1984:8–16, 43). Collective action theorists generally assume, however, that individuals know the prevailing climate of opinion concerning the appropriateness of collective activity. The general knowledge that the Pareto optimal point exists, and is unreachable, provides the "sting" for the general Prisoners' dilemma problem. In both cases, the authors declare this knowledge to be irrelevant to the individual's calculation of his rational strategy. Mancur Olson specifically states that without coercion or selective incentives, individuals in large groups will not contribute to collective goals, "even where there is unanimous agreement in a group about the common good and the methods of achieving it" (Olson, 1965:2). We thus assume that the climate of opinion unanimously favors collective action, following the collective action theorists. There is no question where the Collective stands on this issue.

This assumption was implied on a more general level in chapter 3, when we discussed the location of the Pareto optimal point, given the choice of "all pay" or "none pay" for the collective good or action. Clearly, the former choice is optimal for all individuals; all are better off if all contribute to collective action than if none contribute. Each person receives back in benefits more than he invests in costs. But these two choices do not exhaust all the possible outcomes. Each individual in the group also prefers the condition where all others besides him pay (alternative w in my previous analysis) to the condition where none pay (alternative x). It is possible—and indeed, critical—to define the climate of opinion concerning each of these alternatives for my present analysis.

In the problem of collective action, each individual in the group would opt for alternative w (in which all others pay for the good and he does not) over all other alternatives. If all individuals choose this alternative, the group ends up at outcome x, in which the collective good is not provided or the collective action not taken. Let us now reconstruct the climate of opinion that each individual faces as he makes these choices. Each individual desires that everyone else pay for the collective good. Hence, if we divide our group into Hardin's Individual and the Collective, the Individual is always faced with a unanimous opinion among other group members that he should contribute to the collective goal. His "social utility" lies in the direction of contribution and cooperation (since the Collective defines the fashionable behavior for the individual). Because every individual is faced with a similar climate of opinion, the "social utility" for each individual in the group lies in the direction of payment, or cooperation, toward the collective action.

There is thus a conflict between each person's private and social utilities built into the collective action model, in groups of more than two persons. The critical variable for this conflict is not whether the group feels all individuals should pay; the critical variable is whether the population generally believes the collective action promotes a positive net return for group members. If this belief exists, then a conflict between the private and social utilities of each person in the group also exists.[5]

How will this conflict be resolved? From the model in the previous section concerning individual responses to fashion, the individual's social utility will outweigh his private utility: he will take the fashionable path and contribute to the collective goal. Admittedly, we are dealing with the purest theoretical case here; in real-life situations, we deal instead with tendencies. Furthermore, many factors may affect the individual's calculation of his social utility, including his perceptions of the climate of opinion, the strength of group opinion on the issue, the extent to which contribution is a public act, and the sensitivity of the individual to the threat of isolation. It is best, however, to develop this pure theoretical case through Olson's, Hardin's, and Schelling's models of collective action before introducing such caveats. If our assumptions so far are taken as valid general rules, then it will always be rational for individuals to support collective action approved by the majority.

REFORMULATING THE LOGIC OF COLLECTIVE ACTION

Mancur Olson's formula for the logic of collective action consists of three elements: cost of the collective good (C), total benefits to individual i from the good (V_i), and net benefits from the good when costs of contribution are considered (A_i). Net benefits equal total benefits minus costs, or $A_i = V_i - C$. If $A_i > 0$ for some i, the group will probably succeed, and is defined as privileged. However, if $A < 0$ for all individuals i, the group is latent, and will not succeed without coercion or selective incentives to induce contribution (Olson, 1965:34, 49–50). Olson applies this formula to such organizations as labor unions, farm lobbies, professional associations, and others.

This formulation changes with the inclusion of the social utility of avoiding isolation, C'. Four possible values for A result, depending upon the majority opinion concerning collective action, and the individual's subsequent behavior:

If the majority *approves* of collective action, the individual who *cooperates* receives a reward of $A_i = V_i - C + C'$, or the net benefit described by Olson, plus the social utility of avoiding isolation.   **(1a)**

If the majority *approves* of collective action, the individual who *does not cooperate* receives a reward of $A_i = V_i$, or his share of the collective benefit, with neither the costs nor the utility of avoiding isolation included in the equation.   **(1b)**

Since $C' > C$, $V_i - C + C' > V_i$. Hence, it is always in the individual's interest to contribute to collective action which is approved by a majority of group members.

If the majority *disapproves* of collective action, the individual who *does not cooperate* receives a reward of C', or the utility of avoiding isolation.   **(2a)**

If the majority *disapproves* of collective action, the individual who *cooperates* receives a reward of $A_i = V_i - C$.[6]   **(2b)**

Hence, it is usually in the individual's interest not to contribute to collective action that is not approved by the majority of group members.

Groups are privileged if a majority of group members approve of collective action; groups will tend to be latent when a majority of group members disapprove of collective action.[7] Note, however, that the latter category of groups will only tend to be latent; whether or not they are actually latent depends upon the value of V_i for individual members of the group. Recall that noncontributors in the second set of cases receive a reward of $V_i - C$. Contribution would thus be rational for the individual if $V_i > C' + C_i$ or if his benefit outweighed the cost of providing the good, plus the isolation he would incur for providing a good not explicitly approved by the majority. This case is probably unlikely; indeed, it is more unlikely than in Olson's original formulation, where groups were privileged if $V_i > C$ for any member of the group. But this situation is not impossible, and may in fact arise. Barry and Hardin cite the example of Howard Hughes, who wished to watch westerns and aviation movies on television through the night, despite the fact that his local television station ended programing at 11 P.M. At the station manager's exasperated suggestion, Hughes bought the station and provided his favorite all-night programing. A potential audience of a quarter of a million were a large privileged group who benefited from his decision. (*Time*, April 8, 1974:2; cited in Barry and Hardin, 1982:26).

This story does provide a colorful example of an individual whose private benefit exceeded the cost of providing the collective good (in this case 24-hour programing). But this example illustrates a second point germane to my present analysis. For *Time* did not include this anecdote in its story on Hughes's life because Hughes provided the public with a collective good; such actions are common for philanthropists and usually merit only brief mention. The interest of the story lies in the collective good he chose to supply and his reasons for choosing it; both features illustrate Hughes's eccentricity, his lack of concern with his public image. Imagine, for example, if Hughes had instead contributed $3.8 million (the cost of the television station) to public television in the United States, considering it to be a worthwhile institution; such an action would hardly have merited attention, since public television is generally regarded as a public good worthy of support by most potential viewers in the United States. Hughes's story was noteworthy (and newsworthy) because he provided a collective good to potential viewers without regard for what the viewers desired. (Recall that Hughes programed the 11 P.M. to 6 A.M. time slot according to *his* tastes and not the tastes of the viewing public.) Such action, even when it involves providing a collective good individuals may accept or reject as they please, is sufficient to label the provider an "eccentric," a person who acts with little regard for how others view his behavior. In Locke's terms, he is the one man in ten thousand who acts without consideration of others' opinions (Locke, 1894, 1:476, 479; quoted in Noelle-Neumann, 1984:70). The fear of isolation should make such actions even rarer than Olson's formula predicts, even for the most altruistically minded individuals. The quality V_i must not only exceed the cost of providing the collective good (C) in this case, but also the utility of avoiding isolation (C') that one foregoes in providing the good; hence, V_i must exceed $C + C'$.

Russell Hardin describes a more complex version of this problem, including the benefits and costs individuals incur by contributing to collective action within a group of size N, with a fixed cost/benefit ratio, r (Hardin, 1971:474–77). The preceding conclusions also apply to Hardin's model. Let us adopt Hardin's assumption that $r = 2$; that is, for each unit of the collective good an individual buys, two units of collective benefit are produced. This collective benefit must be divided evenly among all group members, whether they have contributed to the good or not. Assume further that m members in the group contribute to the collective good (which has a cost of C for each contributor), and that $C = 1$. From Hardin's analysis, the net rewards for contributors and noncontributors are as follows:

For contributors, rewards equal their portion of the collective good, minus the cost of contributing, or $A_i = 2(m)/N - C$, where $C = 1$.

Table 1
Payoffs to individual i, where $r = 2$, and $C = 1$, excluding social utility, C'

NUMBER WHO PAY BESIDES $\underline{i}$ ($\underline{N}$ = 10)

		9	8	7	6	5	4	3	2	1	0
	pays	1.0	.8	.6	.4	.2	0	-.2	-.4	-.6	-.8
Payoff to $\underline{i}$ if $\underline{i}$												
	does not pay	1.8	1.6	1.4	1.2	1.0	.8	.6	.4	.2	0

Source: This table is reproduced from Hardin, 1971: 426.

For noncontributors, rewards will equal their portion of the collective good alone, since they pay no costs, or $A_i = 2(m)/N$.

Within the boundaries of Hardin's analysis, the rational individual should not pay; his reward for nonpayment is always higher than his reward for payment, regardless of how many others contribute to the collective good. The payoff matrix for a ten-person group from Hardin's work is shown in Table 1.

It is useful to present these results graphically, in the form used by Thomas Schelling in *Micromotives and Macrobehavior* (1977). Here we present two lines: the solid line represents the net reward for individual i who does not pay, while the broken line represents the net reward for individual i who does pay. The reward (represented on the Y axis) for payment is always lower than the reward for nonpayment, regardless of how many persons (represented on the X axis) pay. The only exception to this rule is if no one pays, in which case no one receives any net rewards, nor pays any costs. This graph is presented in Figure 3.

How does our previous analysis affect the calculation of individuals' dominant strategies within this more formal ten-person model? Once again, individual rewards may be described in terms of four sets of values, depending upon whether a majority supports collective action or not. Assume that a majority supports the collective action if the individuals who comprise the majority contribute to it.[8] When the number of persons contributing exceeds $N/2$, or six persons in a ten-person group, a majority approves the collective action. The location of C' is defined by observing the number of people who contribute in this model. Payoffs are defined as follows:

If a majority feels it is appropriate to contribute, then contributors will receive a payoff of $2(m)/N + C' - C$, or $2(m)/N + C' - 1$, where $C = 1$. (Note that we continue to assume $C' > C = 1$).   **(1a)**

Figure 3
Payoffs to individual i, where $r = 2$, $C = 1$, and $N = 10$, excluding social utility C'

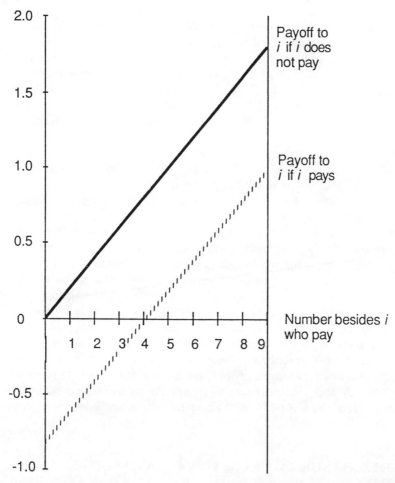

If a majority feels it is appropriate to contribute, then non-contributors receive a payoff of $2(m)/N$, since they do not receive the utility of avoiding isolation. **(1b)**

Because $C' > 1$, $C' - C > 0$; hence, it is once again in the individual's interest to contribute to the cost of collective action that is approved by the majority.

If a majority feels it is not appropriate to contribute, then contributors receive a payoff of $2(m)/N - C$, or $2(m)/N - 1$, since they do not receive the utility of avoiding isolation. **(2a)**

If a majority feels it is not appropriate to contribute, then non-contributors receive a $2(m)/N + C'$, since they avoid isolation but pay no costs.   (2b)

Clearly, individuals should not contribute to the cost of collective action that is not approved by the majority.

In order to reproduce Hardin's payoff matrix for the ten-person group, including the utility of avoiding isolation in the appropriate positions, assume that $C' - C = a$, $C' = 1 + a$, and $a > 0$. To take two examples, $2(m)/N + C - C' = 2(m)/N + a$, while $2(m)/N + C' = 2(m)/N + 1 + a$. The payoff matrix in Table 2 shows the results of this restructuring of rewards.

The results concur with the previous revision of Olson's logic of collective action. The individual should pay if a majority supports collective action; the individual should not pay if a majority does not support collective action. These results are presented graphically in Figure 4, following Schelling's format.

It is necessary at this point to retreat somewhat from this "pure" theoretical case by introducing a few of the caveats mentioned earlier. It is unlikely that all individuals will suddenly adjust their behavior once a majority approves of collective action. Indeed, the spiral of silence theory describes a slow change in behavior as the first step in a process that culminates in a general tendency of minority individuals to fall silent. But the likelihood of individuals exchanging their private utility for the social utility of avoiding isolation depends upon the cost and two other factors described in Noelle-Neumann's work: the individuals' perception of the strength of the threat of isolation (Noelle-Neumann, 1984:42–50) and the individuals' sensitivity to the threat of isolation (Noelle-Neumann, 1984:24–29). These factors are included in the model in the next section.

THE EXCHANGE VALUES OF PRIVATE AND SOCIAL UTILITY

Hardin acknowledges that his definition of "rationality" excludes considerations of "social utility," clarifying the difference between his approach and the approach to "rationality" used in this book:

There is a commonplace meaning of "rationality" that is used in wider contexts, but which I do not use here. Crudely stated, it is that one is rational if, after considering all of one's concerns—moral, altruistic, familial, narrowly self-interested, and so forth—one then chooses coherently in trading off each against the others, or even in refusing to make certain trade-offs. Another way of conceiving of this notion is to suppose that one's mind is compartmentalized, that

Table 2
Payoffs to individual i, where $r = 2$ and $C = 1$, including social utility, $C' - C = a$

NUMBER WHO PAY BESIDES $\underline{i}$ ($\underline{N} = 10$)

	9	8	7	6	5	4	3	2	1	0
Payoff to $\underline{i}$ if $\underline{i}$ pays	2.0 + a	1.8 + a	1.6 + a	1.4 + a	1.2 + a	0	-.2	-.4	-.6	-.8
does not pay	1.8	1.6	1.4	1.2	1.0	1.8 + a	1.6 + a	1.4 + a	1.2 + a	1.0 + a

Majority supports collective action

Majority opposes collective action

Figure 4
Payoffs to individual i, where $r = 2$, $C = 1$, $N = 10$, including social utility C' where $C' - C = a$

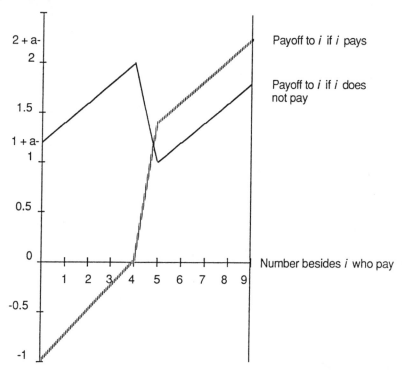

one is a synthesis of several selves, each concerned with an overall regulator who, in making present choices on how to act, assigns systematic weights to all selves, *according as they have already been more or less satisfied. One could meaningfully say of such a regulator that it was rational or irrational. My use of "rational" in this work is less profound and less interesting than such an alternative. I merely use rational to mean "efficient in serving one's self-interest."* . . . Indeed, at issue throughout the analysis . . . is the extent to which behavior that is extrarational in this narrow sense would affect or evidently does affect outcomes in collective action situations. (Hardin, 1982:10–11; emphases mine)

To relax the assumption that $C' > C$ for all individuals once the majority favors contribution is to discuss the tendencies of individual actors who detect a shift in opinion in the society.[9] The discussion of tendencies remains the proper topic of social science research. Some individuals need only perceive a relatively small threat of isolation before they will expend resources to avoid it, while other individuals must perceive a greater threat of isolation before they will make such "defensive expenditures." In Noelle-Neumann's study of controversial subjects, she discovered that lower status groups in the population (that is, the less educated and those employed in lower status positions) were less likely to discuss controversial issues with a fellow train passenger than those of higher status groups (that is, the more educated and those employed in higher status positions) (Noelle-Neumann, 1984:27). Individual characteristics affect a person's decision to avoid or risk isolation. These decisions necessarily include the payment or nonpayment of defensive expenditures.

Another variable in this formulation is the perceived threat of isolation. Noelle-Neumann's analysis indicates that the stronger and more explicit the threat, the more likely individuals are to behave in a manner to avoid isolation (Noelle-Newmann, 1984:422–50). The strength of the perceived threat is related to the proportion of individuals in the population who approve of the collective action, in two ways. First, as more people approve of the action, individuals are more likely to perceive that "most people" approve of the action (recall that the sum of individual opinions and the climate of opinion tend to covary over time, as stated in Proposition III). Second, as more individuals approve of the action, the dissenting individual feels more isolated; small majorities create a smaller threat of isolation to the dissenting individual than larger majorities. For these reasons, the perceived threat of isolation varies with the number of people who support an action in the population.

The cost of avoiding isolation (or the private utility one must give up or forego to serve their social utility) is also a relevant factor in my analysis. Actions that entail relatively low costs, such as walking on a footpath rather than the short way across the grass, would be more amenable to the threat of isolation than actions that entail relatively heavy costs in terms of property, freedom, or life. The latter might be sacrificed to avoid isolation, but it would undoubtedly require a stronger threat of isolation then if the costs were minimal.

Different individuals make different trade offs between their private and social utilities in combining these three factors. In order to graphically conceptualize these exchanges, let the perceived strength of the threat of isolation form the Y axis and the net profit gained from nonconformity (or noncontribution) form the X axis. These two values are represented by C' and C, or the individuals' social and private utilities, respectively. The quantity C equals the profit gained from *not* contributing to the collective action, or the cost incurred if one pays for the action. The graphic representation parallels a procedure applied by Barry concerning trade offs between general political principles:

I wish to maintain that one can sensibly speak of rational choices on the basis of principles which are not all reducible to a single one provided that the (actual or hypothetical) choices made show a consistent pattern of preference. *We can*

best begin by looking at our everyday choices as consumers, for it is in this connection
that the kind of answer I want to give has been elaborated.

When I decide whether to spend a marginal sixpence on grapes or potatoes
. . . must I be able to refer them both to some common yardstick before my choice
can be regarded as rational? The classical answer would be that a rational consumer tries to "maximize his utility" where utility is thought of as a psychological
quantity (pleasure or satisfaction). But the answer that would be favored most
by economists now would be to say that a pattern of choices can be regarded
as rational provided it is consistent. "Consistency" means not just that one
chooses three grapes and four potatoes whenever the choice is open (unless one
admits to a change in taste) but also that one prefers five grapes and three
potatoes to four grapes and three potatoes. Whatever may be the case with
grapes and potatoes this idea seems to me eminently suitable for application to
political principles. Suppose that we imagine there to be only two very general
principles which we may call "equity" and "efficiency" . . . Then for each person
who evaluates in terms of these principles we can draw up a set of indifference
curves showing along each line different combinations of the two between which
he would be indifferent. (Barry, 1965:4–5; emphases mine)

Let us substitute "the perceived strength of the threat of isolation" (the
social utility C') for "equity" and the "profit gained from nonconformity"
(the net gain C) for "efficiency" in Barry's description. Let us also consider the curves he describes as functions defining the exchange rates
of C' and C for individuals in our sample.[10] This procedure is particularly
suited to the present model, since this portion of the investigation began
with a discussion of consumer behavior, the same starting point Barry
uses for his formulation. Label the exchange curves 1, 2, and 3 for three
hypothetical sets of individuals associated with these curves. The curves
represent the trade offs between private and social utilities made by the
respective individuals. Assume further that the curves have the shape
shown in Figure 5.

This graph may be read to compare individuals' reactions to social
isolation regarding collective action with a cost of C (labelled C_i on the
graph). Individuals on curve 3, for example, are indifferent between
incurring isolation and gaining the profit C_i when $C' = C_3'$. If the perceived threat of isolation exceeds C_3', individuals in this set will pay C_i
to avoid it. Individuals on curve 2 have a higher tolerance for the threat
of isolation, being indifferent between the two utilities only when $C' =
C_2'$. If $C' > C_2'$, both sets of individuals (on curves 2 and 3) will pay C_i
to avoid isolation. Finally, individuals on curve 1 have the highest tolerance to the perceived threat of isolation, being indifferent only when
$C' = C_1'$. If $C' > C_1'$, we would expect all three sets of individuals in
our model to pay C_1 to avoid isolation.[11]

This graphic treatment also provides other insights into these exchanges. If $C_1 = 0$ for all values of C' for a given individual, that person

Figure 5
Exchange curves for private and social utility for three individuals

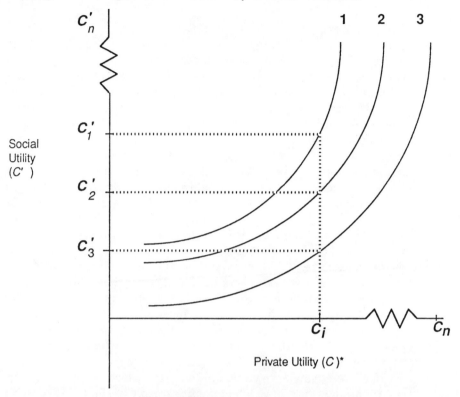

*Note: The private utility is equal to the cost (C)
of contributing to collective action that one
avoids by not paying

would never yield any private gain, regardless of the perceived threat
of isolation. He would be a social leper (or, in fact, an Arrovian dictator),
who always acts without regard for the opinions of others. If $C' = 0$ for
all values of C for a given individual, that person would exist only to
serve others' wishes. He would be a social martyr, who acts only with
regard for the opinions of others. In economic behavior, as in all other
forms of social relations, exchange curves tend to fall somewhere in
between the two extremes. This insight recalls the earlier conclusion that
neither pure private utility nor pure social utility actually exist above
the subsistence level, although economic analysts tend to emphasize the
former and neglect the latter. In a sense, the extremes on this graph
recall Aristotle's statement that an individual who exists outside of civil

society must be either a beast or a god (Aristotle, 1962). Human experience tends to fall between the completely self-serving or self-sacrificing extremes.

Two other extreme values of interest are C_n and C_n'. The quantity C_n represents a cost so high that no individual will pay, regardless of the perceived threat of isolation. None of the curves reach this hypothetical point on the X axis. Similarly, C_n' represents a degree of social isolation so high that individuals will pay any cost to avoid it. None of the curves reach this hypothetical point on the X axis. Similarly, C_n' represents a degree of social isolation so high that individuals will pay any cost to avoid it. None of the curves reach this hypothetical point on the Y axis. Examples of these extremes are also hard to describe, although some cases might approximate these values. If only one person could obtain or possess nuclear weapons, it is unlikely that any degree of social isolation could compel him to join others in foreswearing them, as in the first value, C_n.[12] A soldier who will not desert his fellows under fire, even when it means certain death to remain, might be an example of the second case.[13] These or similar situations might be important in certain contexts, but their occurrence is so rare that it is not useful to discuss them along with most conventional social choices.[14]

Perhaps the most useful conclusion for further analysis is that the higher the value of C', the more likely most or all individuals will pay a given cost C to avoid isolation, and satisfy this social utility. But C' is a function of the *proportion* of individuals in a group who favor collective action. Consider for example, those individuals in the group who have exchange curves similar to curve 3. If enough persons support the collective goal, the threat of isolation might exceed C_3'. Hence, all persons with exchange curves similar to curve 3 will contribute to the collective goal. But the action of this group of individuals increases the proportion of persons publicly supporting the goal. The perceived threat of isolation is thus increased for noncontributors. If this threat increases to the point where it exceeds C_2', then persons with exchange curves similar to curve 2 will also tend to pay. Here, we can see how the perceived threat of isolation increases support for collective action, which in turn increases the perceived threat of isolation above its previous value. If the process continues until it includes the entire group, the spiral of silence is complete: all will eventually contribute, barring any changes in opinion.

These changes can be measured as Noelle-Neumann measured the threat of isolation on other issues. The "perceived threat of isolation" is reflected in the proportion of the population that feels that "most people" support the collective goal. Individual support for collective action should tend to increase with the increase in the perceived threat of isolation. The climate of opinion regarding collective action should covary with support for it, as stated in Proposition III.

Indeed, groups attempt to manipulate this perceived fear of isolation to their own advantage, in order to induce individuals to contribute to a collective good. Consider the case of public television in the United States. Barry and Hardin, in their discussion of this example can only explain public television's existence by arguing that managers solicit funds by convincing viewers that they receive more in value than they pay in the cost of contribution (Barry and Hardin, 1982:121). The authors neglect to mention, however, the custom such stations have of showing a running tally of contributions while employees are soliciting funds. The reason for this tally is obvious: the station wishes to promote the impression that "all others are contributing" and that the noncontributing viewer is therefore socially isolated. This is, of course, just an illusion, given that huge numbers of viewers are free riders not being tallied on the station's display. However, this ploy appears to be an effective fund-raising tool, judging from its general use during televised drives.

The process described above could also easily reach an equilibrium point short of total silencing of nonsupporters or noncontributors, however. Consider again the groups of individuals with exchange curves described by curves 1, 2, and 3. It is entirely possible that the perceived threat of isolation could exceed C_3', but not reach C_2', even when the individuals on curve 3 are included among the contributors. In this instance, some individuals in the group would contribute to the collective goal (that is, those below the C_2' value), while others would not (that is, those above the C_2' value). The equilibrium point between contributors and noncontributors is thus different, and harder to define, than the equilibrium point in Hardin's and Olson's models of collective action. Hardin argues that the only equilibrium point in Olson's model of collective action is where no one will contribute unless coercion is applied (Hardin, 1982:134). Olson states it is possible that collective action will occur at levels lower than full, or almost full, cooperation, but only when it is in one individual's interests to supply the collective good himself; here, the good is supplied at "suboptimal levels" (Olson, 1965:27–32). My preceding analysis offers another explanation for the varying levels of collective activity in different groups.

What general statements may be made about the pattern of contribution or noncontribution for group members in the model, then? Barry places sharp limitations upon the general rules one might derive from his graphic treatment of the trade offs between "equity" and "efficiency," since these concepts cannot be quantified as "grapes and potatoes" are in economic exchanges. However, because one can say a given state is more or less "equitable" or "efficient," these separate principles may, to some extent, be substitutable (Barry, 1965:6). Barry's limitations are less restrictive in the present model, since a reasonable

measure for the strength of the perceived threat of isolation does exist
for any given time: the perception of the climate of opinion. This measure
provides a rough-and-ready rule that may be applied in certain contexts
to predict the relative level of collective action toward a particular goal.
For the more individuals who believe "most people" support contributing to a collective goal, the more individuals will tend to feel isolated
for not contributing. Similarly, the more individuals who believe "most
people" support the collective goal, the stronger the threat of isolation
for noncontributors. The perceived climate of opinion thus has a twofold
effect on the proportion of persons supporting collective action; it affects
the number of people who feel isolated for noncontribution, and it affects
the degree of isolation they are likely to feel. These conclusions define
hypotheses regarding the likelihood of collective action, under conditions of constant costs and benefits for group members:

Hypotheses   The perceived climate of opinion regarding collective action
should tend to covary over time with the actual climate of opinion regarding collective action; it should also therefore covary with the proportion of people contributing to the collective goal. Hence: (a) the
proportion of people who state "most people" support the action should
covary with the proportion of people who say "I support the action;"
(b) the greater the proportion of people who say "Most people support
this action," the more likely individuals are to contribute to it; and (c)
the greater the proportion of people who say "I support this action,"
the more likely individuals are to contribute to it.

Part (a) of these hypotheses is no surprise, since it follows quite explicitly from Proposition III in the first chapter. But this conclusion is
significant for the problem of collective action. Hardin's model proved
that if I consider only my private utility, my interests are increasingly
advanced the greater the number of people who cooperate. The reward
for not paying increases the more individuals contribute to the collective
good. Hence, if I believe that "most people" support the collective goal
and will contribute to it, that should be a strong disincentive against my
cooperation. But, part (a) states that the number of people who approve
of the collective action is related to the number of people who believe
"most people" support this action.
Of course, expressed support for an action is not the same as contributing money to it. Hypotheses (b) and (c) address this point, by
describing contribution as affected by the climate of opinion and the
perception of the climate of opinion. This is a controversial point and
deserves further explanation. First, the distinction between expressing
support for the goal and actually paying for it may not be as clear as
claimed above. If citizen approval is tallied by policy makers who survey

public opinion to guide their actions, then a mere expression of opinion can constitute a contribution to collective action. Because such activities as treaty negotiations or the creation of government regulations often involve commitments to collective goals for a nation's citizens, and because these decisions are often made at the highest governmental levels, it is likely that politicians would keep a close eye on the opinion polls to test whether these actions will be accepted. Approval alone might therefore entail high costs, in terms of collective commitments, for citizens in this case.

But what about contributions that involve direct transfers of time, funds, or energy from the contributor? The earlier references to fashion indicate that contributions to collective action should become more likely when the climate of opinion favors those contributions. Participation in collective activity is a form of individual reaction to fashion or public opinion. In Hirsch's terms, contributions to collective action should become a "defensive expenditure" when the climate of opinion favors such expenditures. This issue will be considered at greater length in the next chapter with reference to Hardin's analysis of mass political and social movements.[15]

This second idea follows from the analysis of exchange curves between private and social utilities. Assume that sensitivity to the threat of isolation is more or less randomly distributed in a given population. Hence, as more individuals believe "most people" support collective action, or as more individuals support the collective action themselves, more people in the group will be sensitive enough to the threat of isolation to contribute to the goal. As more people contribute, the threat of isolation would increase further for noncontributors, since contribution often has clear public effects displaying the action's success. A level may thus be reached where most, or nearly all, persons will contribute, or an equilibrium point may be reached short of this level.

There are, however, certain important limits to this analysis. The hypotheses only allow us to compare the likelihood that a given action with consistent costs and benefits will occur over time, or to compare (in a rough manner) the relative likelihood of two actions with similar costs and benefits occurring at a given time. The analysis does not provide units of "social utility" by which the likelihood of one action (say voting) can be compared with another action (say contributing to a lobbying group) when costs and benefits are dissimilar. The latter comparison requires the assumption that a set value of the fear of isolation, C', exists and has a somewhat predictable effect across several values of C. If it were possible to draw exchange curves for individuals, this assumption might be safe. Since exchange curves are theoretical constructs, such calculation is not possible. Even within these limitations, however, the hypotheses challenge many conventional notions about the likelihood of successful collective action and the possibilities of reaching a generally acceptable conclusion to the Arrow problem. These notions will be discussed further in chapters 6 and 7.

CONCLUSION

It is useful here to summarize the arguments advanced in this chapter. I began by arguing that the expression of preferences in the marketplace follows a pattern similar to the expression of preferences in other forms of social behavior; hence, both should be susceptible to the public opinion processes described in the spiral of silence theory. Fred Hirsch's *Social Limits to Growth* illustrated how one economist dealt with the "source" of consumer choices in the market; we traced the process of "positional competition" described by Hirsch to Noelle-Neumann's theory of public opinion. Next, notions of "private" and "social" utility were shown to be interdependent. When reactions to fashion were considered as a collective action problem, this behavior was incomprehensible without some notion of "social utility" built into the economic model. The rest of the chapter dealt with the effects of this "social utility" upon collective action models that draw their inspiration from the economic model. First, the calculation of one's interests in collective action changed drastically through Olson's, Hardin's, and Schelling's descriptions of the problem, once the social utility, C', was considered in individual actions. Second, this argument was translated into three hypotheses that may be tested empirically.

These hypotheses will now be applied to certain classic problems that follow from the logic of collective action and the Arrow problem. The applications are divided into two parts. The first part, included in chapter 6, uses survey data to test the hypotheses through such examples as contributing to environmental protection, deciding to vote, labor union activity, and others. The second part, included in chapter 7, introduces some qualitative analyses, which advance a redefined notion of "social preference" implied by the hypotheses. Questions to be examined in chapter 7 include how the problem of cyclical majorities may be overcome or ignored in everyday decisions, how the Prisoners' dilemma may be restructured to permit a solution, how institutions take shape to reach legitimate collective decisions, and why democratic systems that embrace majority rule as a privileged rule also tend to embrace values such as fairness and equality.

NOTES

1. I am grateful to Anna Jaeckel for presenting this formal depiction of the combination of these processes in a critique of Kenneth Arrow.

2. I use the terms "public" and "social" interchangeably in this chapter with reference to the values Hirsch describes.

3. Recall the discussion in chapter 2, regarding opinion leaders.

4. Please note that I have retained the previous convention of presenting Row's (or the Individual's) benefit first in the parentheses and Column's (or Collective's) benefit second in the parentheses for each of the alternatives listed.

5. Indeed, it is worthwhile to note that *any* rule that is privileged and responsive will produce the same climate of opinion, not just the unanimous rule. This follows because the problem of collective action is an Arrow problem with a Pareto optimal alternative explicitly added into the cycle of preferences, as noted in the previous chapters. It also follows because any rule that is privileged and responsive will require a majority of the group members to approve collective action, so that the individual is always faced with a majority (or more) of the group who advocate his contribution to the collective goal.

6. This point is particularly important, for it allows us to distinguish between individuals who are motivated to contribute to the collective good out of altruism from individuals who are motivated to contribute in order to avoid isolation. The former should contribute in the case of (2b) above, in the hope that enough others will contribute to create the good, or altruistic individuals might contribute in this case just because it makes them "feel good" to give to a group cause. The latter individuals, who are motivated by the desire to avoid isolation, will not contribute in this case, however, since their contributions were not altruistically motivated in the first place.

7. Note here that I substitute "contribution to the provision of the collective good" for the special case of the individual who "pays the entire amount for the collective good," as described by Olson. I assume here that all individuals are asked to make similar contributions to the collective good; I take up the issue of asymmetries in contributions to the collective good in chapter 7.

8. Note that I am not stating that a majority must contribute before we know a majority supports collective action; rather, I am stating that if a majority does contribute, we can assume that it supports this action. It is the majority approval that precedes their actions that defines the climate of opinion.

9. I am grateful to Bernd Niederman for making this point about the relative values of C and C' in a critique of Thomas Schelling's work.

10. As such, these curves represent a slightly different notion from the indifference curves described by Barry. The notion of "exchange curves" is more suited to my analysis, although the two concepts are similar.

11. I should note that the depiction of these curves is for illustrative purposes only. As such, there is no reason why the curves cannot cross each other or have very different shapes. Also, one would expect that in a given population there would be innumerable exchange curves that could exist in the space defined by the X and Y axes; individuals certainly need not cluster on curves as in my illustration.

12. One might add the caveat here, though, that such weapons are of limited utility, unless one uses them or is prepared to use them. As such, they might be of little help in the everyday relations the possessor has with others. Prospero, one recalls, did bury his book at the end of *The Tempest*.

13. Although individuals might postpone this decision by believing they might, by some means, escape the cost.

14. Indeed, these choices only serve to underscore how weak social theories often become at the extremes; for just as it is virtually impossible to affix a "value" to a meal for a starving person, so too it is difficult to deal with private and social utilities when the stakes are as high as complete power or certain death. Fortunately, we tend to deal with more sedate cases in the establishment and maintenance of social relations.

15. It is interesting to note, however, that we often do not like to think that our commitment to certain values or causes is linked to the nature of the times. In the movie *The Big Chill*, which features a group of ex-radicals from the 1960s, one of the characters looks back upon their experiences and actions and states with wistful regret, "I hate to think that all we did was just a matter of fashion." A significant factor in our decisions regarding collective action is the nature of the times in which we consider it, despite our (rather unjustified) feeling that such contextual effects trivialize our past commitment to collective goals.

6

Analyses of Collective Behavior under Varying Conditions of Opinion

In chapter 4, the source of paradox or fallacy in the Arrow theorem was discovered and explained by reference to the spiral of silence theory. The application of last chapter's hypotheses to the problem of collective action (and the Arrow problem) should be viewed in a similar manner. For Hardin regards our commonly held views about public opinion and collective behavior to be an example of fallacious reasoning:

Since people cause pollution, we are told, people can stop pollution. The slogan seems to be logically impeccable—and yet it also seems specious. Why? It is logically impeccable because it is factually true in a trivial sense: if enough people would do certain things, which it is physically possible to do, pollution would stop. And it is specious because the intention behind this slogan goes beyond this trivial sense. That intention is more easily captured in another claim, a form with which we are all too familiar: if we wanted to stop pollution we would. This claim is an easy analogue to such commonly valid claims as, "If I wanted another helping, I would take it."

However, the preceding analogy is misleading. Indeed, it is an instance of the fallacy of composition. (Hardin, 1982:1)

J. L. Mackie defines this fallacy in greater detail:

We are committing the fallacy of composition when we argue from the premise that every man can decide how he will act to the conclusion that the human race can decide how it will act (for example, with regard to the rate of increase of population or the choice between war and peace).... (Mackie, 1973:172; quoted in Hardin, 1982)

Hardin introduces two themes already discussed with reference to the Arrow problem. The first theme is that the problem of collective action involves a "fallacy" that depends upon a faulty analogy between individuals and group preferences. The transitive condition, which lies at the heart of Arrow's proof, is presumably a property derived from this analogy. The second theme strikes the related note that there is something generally wrong with the notion of "social preference" in the Arrow problem and the problem of collective action. Indeed, Plott advocates abandoning the notion altogether: "For me, the Arrow theorem demonstrates that the concept of social preference involves the classic fallacy of composition, and it is shocking only because the thoughts of social philosophers from which we have developed our intuitions about such matters are subject to the same fallacy" (Plott, 1982:243). Similarly, Little questions whether any decision procedure should be expected to produce an entity known as a "social welfare function" with the characteristics described by Arrow (Little, 1982:275–76).

These themes underscore the argument in chapter 3 that the problem of collective action is merely a specific instance of the Arrow problem. The response to both of these problems in that chapter implies a different interpretation of the issues raised above. For we are *not* committing a fallacy of composition or setting up a faulty analogy between individual and group preferences in these problems if the spiral of silence theory has general validity. Consider the latter part of Mackie's statement concerning the fallacy of composition: "This, or a similar fallacy, is committed whenever we assume, *without adequate reason*, that we can speak about groups in the same ways in which we speak about their members, that we can speak about a nation having a will or interests" (Mackie, 1973:173; quoted in Hardin, 1982:1; emphases mine). When we "speak" of groups or nations as acting with "one will," or when groups "speak" of themselves in this way, we are dealing with a particular form of speech, expression, and communication. Does the spiral of silence theory provide "adequate reason" for describing such expression as valid? According to Noelle-Neumann's theory, groups may appear to speak as if with one voice, or as if they possessed one interest, because the alternatives are silenced due to the fear of isolation. This insight might explain our tendency to fall into the supposed "fallacy of composition" in this manner.

Let us begin by admitting that we commonly fall prey to this "fallacy" in our analysis of political and social phenomena. To take but one example, all political scientists are familiar with some form of the following litany describing interest group formation:

Three things make a group *politically relevant*: a common interest, awareness of that common interest, and organization. In addition, groups are more likely to be successful in achieving their political goals if they can get their members to give time, spirit, and resources to the group. (Prewitt and Verba, 1983:289; emphases mine)

This statement was drawn from an introductory textbook in American politics; one could no doubt find similar references in countless other texts in political science. These steps in interest group formation are generally recited as if they followed rationally, one upon the other—shared interests can lead to an awareness of shared interests, and this awareness leads to organization. If anything is critical to this process, it is usually viewed as the "consciousness raising" required to move individuals between the first and second steps toward organization.[1]

The collective action theorists would argue otherwise, of course. The problem, they would state, lies instead in the transition from a shared awareness of a common interest to a viable organization. (Recall that Olson claims collective action will not occur under most circumstances even if all members perceive its usefulness.) The collective action theorists' persuasive arguments thus beg the question of why we are so likely to commit such a fallacy, even as Olson's "logic of collective action" has been widely disseminated through the discipline.

The hypotheses from the previous chapter provide a possible explanation. For the first two steps in group formation define a process of public opinion that should, under certain circumstances, promote the third step. Recall that the threat of isolation, C', was related to the number of people who advocated collective action, and to the number of people who believed that "most people" advocated such action. These measures correspond to the individual's perception of his own interest and the general perception that this interest is shared by his peers, respectively. Hence, the first two steps in group mobilization are indicators of the degree of social isolation faced by the individual who does not contribute to action promoting the interests he shares with others in the society.

The hypotheses therefore suggest that, at the least, contribution to collective action should become more likely as more individuals support the action and perceive its increased popularity. This question is particularly suited for empirical analysis. In this chapter, the hypotheses will be tested in a variety of situations suggested by previous analyses of collective action and decision making. These situations include: contributions to environmental protection (discussed in Hardin, 1982:101–102; 106; 221–22); labor union activity (discussed in Olson, 1965:66–97; Barry, 1978:13–46; and Riker and Ordeschook, 1968:26–42); and the problem of cyclical majorities using ranked party choices (discussed most generally in Arrow, 1963; Hardin, 1982:139–42; and Downs, 1957:18, 68).[2]

THE SPIRAL OF SILENCE AND ENVIRONMENTAL PROTECTION

The peculiar case of the Sierra Club, an American organization dedicated to protecting the environment and public lands, occupies Hardin's analysis throughout much of *Collective Action* (Hardin, 1982:101–102; 106, 221–22). The author investigates how the group overcomes the theoretical barriers to collective action to such goals. A similar question arises concerning sentiment and activity for environmental protection within the German Federal Republic, where groups with a comparable—or deeper—commitment to this cause exist. The Greens, a political party whose name derives from its strict positions on the environment, is but one example of the concern West Germans feel about this issue. The evidence suggests that attitudes to environmental protection underwent a profound change in this nation between the years 1970 and 1973. Our hypotheses suggest that a similar change in citizens' willingness to contribute to this cause should have occurred.

Let us first describe those measures that reflect the relative value of C' in the society: the climate of opinion and the perception of the climate of opinion on this issue. The climate of opinion is measured here by a question in which respondents were asked to choose a likely scenario for the future of the environment, if present conditions continued unchecked. The first two scenarios were the most grave, describing conditions under which human life, or plant life, were seriously endangered, respectively; the other two scenarios described less serious effects. In 1970, only 39 percent of respondents described the future using the first two scenarios (with 8% choosing the worst case, and 31% choosing the second worst case). In 1972, however, 66 percent of respondents selected the two worst scenarios (with 14% choosing the worst case, and 52% choosing the second worst case). The proportion of the population viewing this problem with alarm thus changed from a minority in 1970 to a majority in 1973.

This increased individual awareness was apparently matched by an increased group awareness of the problem. In 1970, 55 percent of respondents said they discussed this problem "often" or "sometimes" with others. By 1973, this figure had risen to 78 percent of the population. Another question that directly reflects whether respondents believe the problem is their responsibility, and thus a suitable goal for collective action. In 1970, more respondents believed that pollution was the responsibility of industry (49%) rather than the responsibility of citizens (44%). By 1973, this perception had also changed; a strong majority believed that citizens were responsible for the problem (66%) rather than industry (28%). If the exhortation that "people cause pollution, so people can stop pollution" has any persuasive power, then this power should

Figure 6
Exchange curves when the cost (C) and the threat of isolation (C') vary

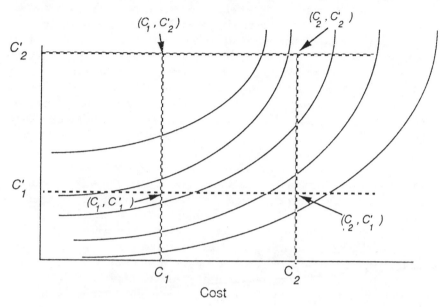

have increased with the growing perception that citizens did, indeed, bear the responsibility for the problem.

The surveys also provide a useful measure of C, or the cost of contributing to collective action to clean up the environment. In 1970 and 1973, respondents were asked if they would contribute varying amounts per month (either 2 DM or 4 DM) to protect the environment. Due to the extra data available concerning the values of C, a more complex analysis of collective action was designed since costs were not a constant value. This analysis required a refining of the exchange curve models used in chapter 5.

Consider again the notion of exchange curves existing for groups of individuals, as shown in Figure 6. If we wish to consider the effects of changes in the threat of isolation (C') and changes in the cost of contributing to collective action (C), we must consider four points on this chart and the position of the individuals' exchange curves relative to these points. Let us first consider the effects if costs were fixed at C_1 and the threat of isolation increased over time from C_1' to C_2'. If $C' = C_1'$, then the number of individuals who would pay C_1 to avoid isolation is represented by the three exchange curves that fall below the point (C_1, C_1'). If C' increased to C_2', then the number of individuals who would pay C_1 to avoid isolation is represented by the five exchange curves that fall below point (C_1, C_2'). A similar logic applies if the cost of contribution rises to C_2. If $C' = C_1'$, then the number of individuals who would pay C_2 to avoid isolation is represented by the one exchange curve which falls below (C_2, C_1'). If C' increases to C_2', then the number of individuals who would pay C_2 to avoid isolation is represented by the three exchange curves that fall below (C_2, C_2'). As the threat of isolation increases, the percentage of individuals willing to pay a specific amount (that is, C_1 or C_2) should also increase.

Next, consider the effects if the threat of isolation were fixed at C_1'. With this threat of isolation, the number of individuals willing to pay C_1 to avoid isolation is represented by the three exchange curves that fall under (C_1, C_1'). The number of individuals willing to pay C_2 to avoid isolation is represented by the one exchange curve that falls under (C_1, C_1'). If the threat of isolation is fixed at C_2', then the number of individuals willing to pay C_1 to avoid isolation is represented by the five exchange curves that fall under (C_1, C_2'). The number of individuals willing to pay C_2 to avoid isolation is represented by the three exchange curves that fall under (C_1, C_2'). For a given threat of isolation, the percentage of individuals willing to pay to avoid isolation decreases as the cost of avoidance increases.

If the hypotheses regarding citizen tradeoffs between C' and C are correct, then these questions should yield two results: the percentage of citizens willing to contribute a specific amount (either 2 DM or 4 DM) should increase with an increased public awareness of the problem and citizens' responsibility for it; and in either year, the percentage willing to contribute 4 DM should be lower than the percentage willing to contribute 2 DM to solving the problem. The results confirm these expectations. First, the percentage of persons willing to contribute 2 DM to the collective goal rose from 42 percent in 1970 to 54 percent in 1973; similarly, the percentage of persons willing to contribute 4 DM increased from 30 percent in 1970 to 36 percent in 1973. Second, the respondents were more likely to contribute 2 DM in either year (41% in 1970, 54% in 1973) than to contribute 4 DM (30% in 1970, 36% in 1973). The proportion of the population willing to contribute to collective action appears to be a function of the values of C and C', as predicted by my hypotheses. Although it is impossible—and as Barry notes, implausi-

Figure 7
Percentage of respondents willing to contribute to environmental protection when costs and climate of opinion vary

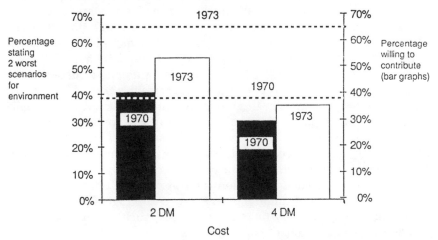

ble—to sketch indifference curves for individuals in the population, the aggregate result of these theoretical curves appears reflected in the responses. These results are presented graphically in Figure 7.

None of the questions used in the following analyses include cases in which the cost of contribution varies. These analyses measure only the changes in collective activity over time when the threat of isolation changes and where costs and benefits of contribution are held constant. However, the application of the models and hypotheses from chapter 5 still apply in these simpler cases.

THE SPIRAL OF SILENCE AND LABOR UNION ACTIVITY

Labor organization in industrialized nations illustrates the power of the threat of isolation for encouraging the existence and growth of unions. Much attention and analysis have been focused upon violence and threats directed against nonunionized laborers as a means of encouraging unionization; yet, the threat of isolation remains a major tool in promoting labor organization. Olson tends to ignore the nonviolent aspects of social coercion in his analysis, focusing instead upon the physical coercion that prompts the growth of unions: "In most cases it is compulsory membership and coercive picket lines that are the source of the union's membership" (Olson, 1965:75). There are two problems with this argument as a primary explanation for unionization, however.

First, as Barry and Hardin point out, compulsory membership in a union seems a product of union organization, not a cause of it (Barry and Hardin, 1982:29). The closed shop follows upon the union's acceptance, not vice versa, and does not account for the organization's existence in the first place. Olson's analysis provides a possible response by stating that unions are often initially created through threats of violence. As he notes, referring to an essay by Daniel Bell, "Violence is apparently the greatest when unions first try to organize a firm" (Olson, 1965:71; see also Bell, 1960:195–97). But this argument is susceptible to Olson's own logic of collective action. Workers who are unlikely to join a union in order to advance their collective interests would seem equally unlikely to join together in violent activity to coerce others to unionize. Of course, it might take a relatively small number of violent unionists to coerce a large number of workers to join the organization. But this action could be met with equal or greater violence by the owners who were trying to avoid unionization (and apparently often was, if one reviews the history of union movements). Without general support for the violence practiced by the trade unionists, such action would seem likely to fail as a means of encouraging organization.

Violence was often successful in encouraging unionization because overt coercion was often coupled with a more subtle coercion: the threat of social isolation. The major reason people avoid crossing a picket line is not the potential violence Olson cites, but rather the verbal abuse and public taunts of striking workers. Similarly, the social pressures to join a union and conform to its work rules are enormous once one begins working in an open, but partially unionized, shop. All of the punishments of social isolation described by Noelle-Neumann—co-workers shunning a person, people moving away from the individual on the street or a bus—are brought to bear upon the dissenter.

An interesting example of this pressure is described by Barry when he discusses the political levies garnered from union members to support the Labor Party in Britain. Barry notes that the levy is more effective when workers must "contract out" of it to avoid payment, instead of having to "contract in" to contribute payment. He finds this difference in effectiveness difficult to explain in terms of collective action theory, arguing that "asking to contract out invites social sanctions from fellow workers . . . but failure to contract in might equally do so." Barry credits the difference in success to inertia—that is, once contribution is a habit, individuals will not tend to go out of their way to stop (Barry, 1978:41). But what Barry credits to inertia here appears instead to be a clear case of the power of the threat of isolation, for contracting out is an individual action that requires separating oneself from one's fellow workers by making the request. The act of "contracting out" explicitly evokes the notion of isolating oneself from others in the union. As Noelle-Neumann notes, individuals are unlikely to risk such an explicit form of isolation.

It is no surprise, then, that "failure to contract in," which does not require an explicit break with an established group, would not evoke the same fear of isolation and would be less successful as a prod toward collective action.

According to our hypotheses, then, unionization should increase as the threat of isolation toward nonunionized workers increases. This threat, in turn, should depend upon the climate of opinion in the society regarding unionization. Assuming that the costs of unionization remain relatively constant over time for workers, unionization should covary with the climate of opinion, representing C' on this issue.

The state of union organization in the United States since the 1950s lends support to this hypothesis. Lipset and Schneider note that there appears to be a relationship between the decline in unionization in the United States and the decline in citizen confidence in unions:

Have unions been affected by the loss of public confidence in them during the 1960s and the 1970s? The evidence on union membership and the results of union elections held by the National Labor Relations Board suggests that they may have.

Except for the immediate postwar period, union membership as a percentage of the nonagricultural labor force reached a high in 1954 when it stood at 35 percent. The favorability rating for labor unions was also very high at that time; the Gallup poll for 1953 shows 75 percent approving of labor unions. Union membership as a percentage of the nonagricultural workforce fell off slightly in the next five years to 33 percent in 1957, the year in which the Gallup approval rating reached an all-time high of 76 percent. Unions' percentage of the labor force began to decline steadily after that. It was at 30 percent in 1961, 25.5 percent in 1975, 24 percent in 1978, 23 percent in 1979, and 21 percent in 1980, the latest figure available. From 1967 to 1980, the percentage belonging to unions and the percentage of the population favorable to unions were going down together. Another indicator of the appeal of unions to American workers is the ability of labor organizations to win elections supervised by the National Labor Relations Board. This trend also seems to reflect a reduced faith in unions. In 1940, unions won 77 percent of organizing elections; in 1950, 74.5; in 1960, 60 percent; the figures stayed at 60 percent in 1965 and 61 percent in 1966. The proportion of union victories then began to fall, down to 55 percent in 1970, 50 percent in 1974, and less than half after that; 48 percent in 1975, 46 percent in 1977, and 45 percent in 1979 and 1980. The decline once again coincides with the period of declining public confidence. (Lipset and Schneider, 1983:353).

As the climate of opinion became less favorable toward unions in the United States, their membership and influence on National Labor Relations Board elections declined. These trends covary despite the continued existence of the same selection incentives and coercion Olson associates with early union successes.

An analysis of the American case alone is not a complete test of the

Figure 8
Climate of opinion about unions and union membership

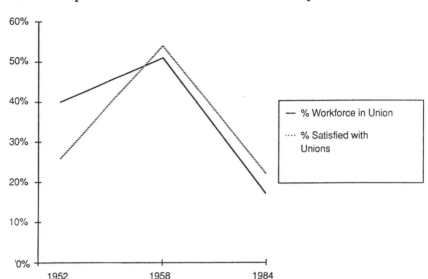

hypotheses, however. Here, we observe a steady decline in union for-
tunes that matches the decline in favorable opinions towards unions.
These declines might possibly be explained within Olson's analysis,
however. Olson implies that an awareness of the appropriateness of
collective action (here, support for unions) is a necessary, but not sufficient condition for collective action. It therefore follows that unionization should not exist if it is considered inappropriate; but this does
not imply that unionization should exist if it is considered appropriate.
While the American data does support the hypotheses, then, it also
might be interpreted as supporting Olson's theory.

West German data suggests, however, that union activity tends to
fluctuate upward as well as downward with similar long-term changes
in the climate of opinion. In 1952, 1958, and 1984, respondents were
asked if they were satisfied that unions operated in their members'
interests. In 1952, 26 percent answered that they were very or somewhat
satisfied with unions in this regard; by 1958, this percentage had risen
to 54 percent, only to fall back to 22 percent in 1984. Membership in
labor unions followed a similar pattern in the Federal Republic, as shown
in Figure 8. In 1952, 40 percent of respondents were union members;
this percentage rose to 52 percent in 1958, then fell to 17 percent in 1984.
Despite short-term fluctuations in these general patterns, union membership seemed to increase or decrease with similar fluctuations in the
climate of opinion regarding unions.

Shifts in the climate of opinion regarding a union's right to compel workers to join the union also appear to be related to the percentage of workers who are unionized. Compelling or coercing workers to join a union is a collective activity or judgment that should be susceptible to the same logic of collective action as unionization itself. Hence, its usefulness as an organizing tool should depend upon the climate of opinion regarding such coercion, as noted above. This hypothesis is supported by the data. In 1952, respondents were asked if all workers should be union members; more than twice as many persons responded positively as negatively (44% versus 20%, respectively). In 1980, however, the climate of opinion was evenly split on this issue with 36 percent responding positively and 35 percent responding negatively. Similarly, respondents also became less willing to force workers to join a union. In 1952, 24 percent agreed that workers should be forced to join a union, while 70 percent disagreed; in 1980, only 13 percent favored compulsory union membership, while 80 percent opposed it. Finally, the percentage of respondents who belonged to unions dropped from 40 percent in 1952 to 21 percent in 1980. Like other forms of collective action, support for coerced union membership fluctuates with the climate of opinion regarding unionization; also, the success of compulsory methods for promoting unionization appears to fluctuate with the climate of opinion regarding the appropriateness of those methods. These results are summarized in Figure 9.

Finally, certain evidence suggests that strikes are more likely to occur in a favorable climate of opinion than in an unfavorable one. In 1963, the climate of opinion regarding strikes in the Federal Republic was generally unfavorable; 53 percent of respondents stated that the government should intervene to end strikes (Allensbach Survey 1077). In 1978, the percentage of respondents approving of government intervention (and hence, disapproving of strikes) fell to 32 percent (Allensbach Survey 3056). Strike activity followed the same pattern; such activity was more common in 1978 than in 1963 by all measures. Strikes were more frequent (1,239 in 1978, as compared with 187 in 1963), more work days were lost (4,201,000 in 1978, as compared with 878,000 in 1963), and more workers participated in strikes (487,000 in 1978, as compared with 101,000 in 1963) in the later year than in the earlier year (*Statistische Jahrbuch*, 1967; 1985). One must, of course, be cautious in interpreting these results. Strike activity is a short-term action, partially dependent upon economic factors not included in this model. Another piece of evidence should be added in this regard, however. A West German analyst compared strike activity under varying conditions for the years 1967 and 1975 and found that even though economic conditions were more suited to strike activity in 1975, strikes were more common in 1967. The author attributes this difference to the mass media; he shows through content analyses that the media reported strikes in a more

Figure 9
Climate of opinion about union obligations and forced membership in unions, and union membership

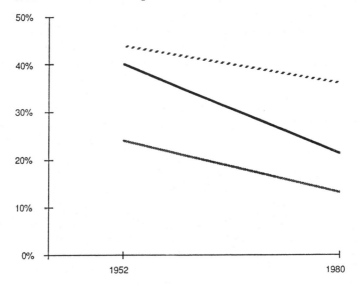

Percentage Stating "All Workers Should Belong to Unions"   · - - - - - -

Percentage Stating "All Workers Should be Forced to Join a Union"   ———

Percentage of Union members in Workforce   ⎯⎯⎯⎯

favorable manner in 1967 than in 1975, thereby encouraging the climate of opinion toward support for this activity (Kepplinger, 1984:71–73). We must, of course, be cautious about assuming that mass media necessarily influences collective activity by affecting the climate of opinion. However, to the extent that reporting affects (or reflects) the climate of opinion, it might be viewed as one indicator of the influence of public opinion upon collective activity.

THE SPIRAL OF SILENCE AND POLITICAL PARTICIPATION

Perhaps one of the most vexing problems in collective action theory concerns the reasons why narrowly rational individuals participate in politics. This question was initially raised in Downs's work on voting, although many of Downs's conclusions apply to other forms of political activity as well, including interest group formation, working on political campaigns, contributing to a political party, and so on (see Downs, 1957:244).

Downs reduces the calculation of whether a rational individual in a two-party contest should vote to two components: his "party differential" (or how much better off he would be if his party won the election) multiplied by the probability that his vote would make the difference between his party winning or losing. Since the chances of one vote making a difference in large populations is virtually nil, even in a close election, the rational person should not vote even if his party differential is very high (Downs, 1957:266–71). The problem with this analysis, however, is that people do vote; even in the United States, where voting is less common than in other liberal democracies, at least 50 percent turn out on election day—a proportion too high to be explained by Downs's calculations.

Downs acknowledges that voting aimed at affecting the election outcome is inexplicable and changes the focus of his argument to the "value of voting *per se*," stating that individuals will vote because they have an interest in the continued existence of the democratic system (Downs, 1957:166). Alas, this argument falls prey to the same problem of rationality as voting to affect one's party's victory. For if one vote is unlikely to make the difference in one party's victory over another, that vote is much less likely to make the difference in supporting continuance of the democratic system since all votes, for either party, would provide support for the system.

Before critiquing this argument as a problem of collective action, we must realize what is at stake here, for we are discussing some of the basic issues of democratic legitimacy raised in chapters 1 and 4. Individuals generally recognize that there is an inherent value in preserving democracy as a choice system (recall Barry's point that democracy will tend to be favored as the best possible choice system for deciding outcomes). The problem is that we may not wish to "pay" the costs of preserving democracy; in chapter 4, I described the costs of complying with decisions that are not in our interests. Voting costs are but another example of the contribution individuals must make to preserve the system. Narrow rationality alone cannot provide a justification for contributing to the "cost" of preserving this choice system, even though this system is generally recognized as the best. Democracy cannot become a privileged rule supported only by individuals' private interests.

How may we focus upon the Prisoners' dilemma problem involved in voting to preserve the democratic system? The spiral of silence theory is easily applied to this problem—all desire that someone else pay the cost of voting in order to preserve the system, and all abstain from voting because they perceive their votes will have little effect upon the system's continued existence. A given citizen is thus faced with a unanimous climate of opinion stating that he should vote, even though he prefers the outcome where all others vote while he abstains. Individuals will thus tend to vote because they fear social isolation if they do not vote.

This explanation requires evidence that two relationships exist in democratic societies: citizens should tend to associate voting with their obligation to the democratic system, and the proportion of people voting should vary with the proportion of people who support the system and who link support for the system with voting. Unfortunately, empirical studies of these relationships are particularly difficult to find; we are forced to make do with the evidence that exists. In an early study, Riker and Ordeshook dealt with the effects of an individual's party differential (low or high), the expected closeness of an election (close or not close), and the individual's sense of "citizen duty" (high, medium, or low) on the respondent's tendency to vote (Riker and Ordeshook, 1968:25–42). They concluded that each of these factors affects a person's decision to vote; however, the evidence shows that "citizen duty" had the greatest effect, and the expected closeness of the election had relatively little effect. These results support the focus upon voting as a "duty" imposed upon the voter. But what is the "citizen duty" that the authors describe here? Alas, the index that measures this concept merely indicates whether voting has a value beyond its effects upon a specific election outcome. The questions do not specify what that value might be:

Citizen duty . . . was measured by a scale composed of several different items which were intended to tap the more important components of this political value. The following four statements (requiring a simple "Agree" or "Disagree" response) were included in the pre-election interview:

1. It isn't important to vote when you know your party doesn't have a chance to win.
2. A good many local elections aren't important enough to bother with.
3. So many other people vote in national elections that it doesn't matter to me whether I vote or not.
4. If a person doesn't care how an election comes out, he shouldn't vote in it.

Obviously, the respondent must disagree with these statements if he is to express feelings of political obligation. He must feel that all elections (national, state, or local) deserve his participation, that neither overwhelming electoral odds nor the apparent insignificance of the single vote should stand as barriers to voting, and indifference to the outcome of a particular election should be no deterrent. (Campbell, Gurin and Miller, 1954:194–95)

Negative responses to these questions, however, merely indicate that voting has a value beyond the citizen's party differential (questions 2 and 4) and his perceived chances of affecting the outcome of the election (questions 1 and 3). But this scale (and the common negative responses to these questions) merely lead us back to the previous conclusion that voting has some value other than its effect upon specific elections, a value that compels individuals to participate. What is this value, and from where do citizens derive the "sense of duty" to vote?

I suggested above that citizen duty arose from a shared sense of obligation to the democratic system in a society where the climate of opinion links support for democracy with voting. Voting is thus reinforced by the sense of isolation nonvoters feel in such a society. West German data seems to support this hypothesis. When citizens were asked "If it is said that someone is a good democrat, which of these characteristics and attitudes would you suspect apply to this person?", the most common response (given by 83% of respondents) was "Votes at every election" (Noelle-Neumann, 1981:135). The percentage of people in the Federal Republic who claimed that they voted regularly in federal, state, and local elections was similarly high at 73 percent (Noelle-Neumann, 1981:152). Unfortunately, there was no data available to compare the attitudes about this form of participation and the rate of voting over time; however, we do have comparable data from the same survey regarding other forms of political activity. These results are presented in Table 3.

As I noted in the previous chapters, one must be careful when comparing activities that entail different costs when evaluating the effects of public opinion upon collective activity. The results in Table 3 must be considered suggestive only. With this caution in mind, however, we can make some preliminary observations about the data. For one could argue that "keeping informed" or "standing up for one's convictions" would generally require less effort and cost than voting, or indeed, that keeping informed was a prerequisite for voting. Yet, these activities are less likely than voting in keeping with their lower association with the actions of a "good democrat."

We should also consider that democratic systems put great effort into encouraging their citizens to vote and attempting to isolate the nonvoter. The effects of such exhortations (and other moral appeals to vote) are reflected in the number of people who claim they voted on public opinion surveys, even if they did not do so. In the 1976 presidential election in the United States, for instance, 54.2 percent of eligible voters went to the polls (Ladd, 1982:60). However, in a subsequent survey by the National Opinion Research Center, 65.7 percent of respondents claimed they voted in this election—a difference well outside the sampling error for the survey (N.O.R.C., 1983:73). Citizens misrepresent their activities because they feel a social pressure to claim they voted even when they did not do so; it is no surprise, then, that other citizens actually do vote to avoid the social stigma attached to nonvoting.

The preceding information only links voting to support for the dem-

Table 3
Democratic characteristics and participation

Characteristics of a "good democrat"	Percentage
"Votes at every election"	83%
"Is well-informed about politics"	75%
"Stands up for his convictions"	49%
"Is a member of many organizations"	13%

Descriptions applying to me	Percentage
"I vote regularly"	73%
"I keep myself well-informed about politics"	46%
"There are political issues which I strongly believe in, and I stand up for my convictions when talking to others"	40%
"I am politically involved in a club. party, or organization"	7%

Source: Noelle-Neumann, 1981: 135, 152.

Figure 10
Participation in European parliamentary elections and opinion about United Europe

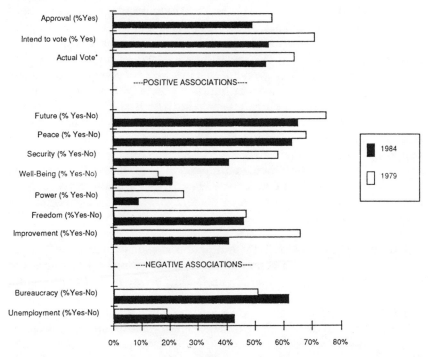

Source: Statistischer Jahrbuch, 1985; p. 88.
All other sources: Allensbach Surveys 3066 (1979); 4040 (1984), 4044 (1984).

ocratic system for one point in time. Data on systematic support over time is difficult to obtain, in part because support for the system does not tend to vary measurably in most cases in established democratic societies. A useful context in which to study varying support levels for such a system might be when that system is in the process of being founded. Such evidence is also difficult to obtain. But we do discover in the West German data an evocative example that suggests a link between support for a democratic system defined by certain boundaries and voter participation.

For the past decade or so, efforts have been made to form a "United Europe" of the Western European nations. Toward this end, a European parliament has been formed in which member nations are represented by delegates elected within the respective countries. Support for this effort was quite high within the Federal Republic in 1979, as shown in Figure 10; 56 percent of the respondents surveyed approved of West German membership in a United Europe of Western European nations.

The percentage of people intending to vote in the European elections (71%) and the percentage actually voting (64%) were also quite high. Between 1979 and 1984, however, the climate of opinion toward a United Europe shifted in the Federal Republic. The percentage of people supporting membership in such an entity fell to 49 percent in the latter year. Similarly, the percentage of respondents associating a United Europe with positive qualities (i.e. "the future," peace, security, well-being, power, freedom, and improvement) fell in seven out of eight cases, while the percentages of people associating such a body with negative qualities (i.e. unemployment and bureaucracy) rose in both cases. Given the early stage of development for this union of nations, participation in European parliamentary elections should also have dropped with this decline in support in West Germany. These expectations are confirmed: the percentage of people saying they would participate in the elections fell from 71 percent to 55 percent between 1979 and 1984, and the percentage of people actually voting fell from 64 percent to 54 percent between these years. Voter participation appeared to fluctuate with support for the system so constituted.

A caveat should be added concerning these results: there is a difference between support for democracy as a means of making social choices and support for a democratic system with specific boundaries. The preceding evidence deals with a specifically defined democratic unit, the support for which may have little to do with the citizens' overall support of majority rule. But discussion of this case is critical to an analysis of voting as an expression of support for a democratic system because of the threat of isolation that underpins this support. One's acceptance of majority rule must be linked to the degree of exposure one feels within the society one is joining; otherwise, the fear of isolation would be less of a threat to individuals within that society, and the pressure to contribute to the society will be lessened. In Noelle-Neumann's terms, public opinion is peculiar to a particular time and place, and moving beyond the social boundaries implied by public opinion at any given time might remove the individual from its influence.

This point has caused many problems with previous analyses of the roots of nationalism within particular countries. Analysts have often tended to assume that if a group or society exists, then a feeling of solidarity or public exists that binds together individuals in the group. This assumption is inherently conservative, for if such ties exist, how does change occur? It also begs the question of how societies come to exist in the first place. Perhaps the most important contribution that the spiral of silence theory makes to this debate is that the fear of isolation is *not* a dependent variable that is assumed within a group. Rather, the fear of isolation is an independent variable that determines the power of the society to influence an individual's decisions. The feeling of "exposure" that underlies the threat of isolation is a phenomenon to be investigated and measured, not assumed, within a society. As Barry implies in the conclusion to "Is Democracy Şpecial?", nationalism and support for a democratic system within certain national boundaries require a general consensus regarding those boundaries—and hence, a general consensus regarding the people inside and outside of those boundaries. This feeling is a critical part of the feeling of exposure to the opinions of one's peers in the truest sense of "public" described in chapter 2. This feeling is also the important variable that determines the boundaries of a democratic unit. The threat of isolation, which makes majority rule a privileged rule, refers as much to the choice system by which decisions are made as to the boundaries within which that system operates.

THE SPIRAL OF SILENCE AND CYCLICAL GROUP PREFERENCES

In chapter 3, I showed how the Prisoners' dilemma and the problem of collective action may be interpreted as specific instances of the general Arrow problem. My application of the spiral of silence theorems to the general problem has been heretofore limited to these specific instances. In this section, I will address the Arrow problem more directly by concentrating on the issue of cyclical group preferences that lies at the heart of Arrow's proof. I begin with an analysis of a context in which cyclical preferences may occur—the ranking of party preferences in the Federal Republic. I then apply the spiral of silence theorems to discover whether voting intentions or party orderings are affected by perceptions of the climate of opinion.

In chapter 4, I took issue with the existence of a dictator whose choices prevail in social decisions, regardless of the preferences of other individuals in the group. The threat of isolation made it unlikely that an individual would express an opinion contrary to the group's choice. Hence, this preference could not become the social preference since it could not be communicated. The relevance of this case for social decision making is severely limited, however. More common, and more serious, is the possibility of cyclical group preferences for persons ranking three or more choices. In this case, a group in the population smaller than the least decisive subset may prevail over a decisive subset if the transitive rule is invoked. If the spiral of silence theorems describe behavior accurately, however, majority rule should tend to be privileged and the transitive rule invalidated.

A conflict between a responsive rule and transitivity may exist only if a group advocating the less popular position in a society claims victory by invoking the transitive rule at some point in the cycle of group preferences. If there is only one decisive subset possible in a society, however, then the rule used to reach decisions must require a majority or more of the population. The group invoking the transitive rule thus faces a majority advocating a different position. Faced with majority opposition, the former group should tend to fall silent.

This conclusion assumes that voting choices or preference rankings among parties are susceptible to the prevailing climate of opinion. The problem of collective action and the problem of cyclical group preferences converge. If voters are less likely to express an unpopular sentiment, just as group members are less likely to dissent from popular collective behavior, then the conflict between responsive and transitive rules is less likely to occur. But are party rankings and voting intentions actually sensitive to changes in the perceived climate of opinion on these issues?

This analysis involves two questions that must be considered separately: does the ranking of party choices in a society tend to covary with the perceived climate of opinion and does voting intention tend to covary with the perceived climate of opinion? Both questions fit easily into the framework of the hypotheses from chapter 5, which postulated that the tendency towards collective action in a society covaries with the perceived and actual climate of opinion. The only difference here is that we are dealing with rankings of voter choices, instead of the decision to contribute or not to collective action and the outcomes these decisions imply.

In order to address these questions empirically, data concerning the three major parties in the Federal Republic (the CDU/CSU, the SPD, and the FDP) were examined for three periods in recent history. In a series of surveys conducted between 1978 and 1979, and between 1980 and 1981, West German citizens were asked to rank these parties in terms of their first, second, and third preferences. Respondents were also asked to evaluate the climate of opinion regarding the two major parties—the CDU/CSU (the right-leaning party) and the SPD (the left-leaning party). The results of the party rankings, and the relationship between rankings and the perceived climate of opinion toward the major parties, have profound implications for the possible conflict between the transitive and majority rules.

Let us recall briefly the analysis from chapter 4, which examined the ideological conditions under which West German politics tends to be conducted. The data from 1979 indicated that first-place party rankings tended to be determined by voters' partisan preferences. Party preferences also tended to be single-peaked among supporters of the CDU/CSU and the SPD. Seventy-six percent of the SPD supporters tended to rank their party first and the CDU/CSU last (since these parties represent the left and right ends of the ideological spectrum in Germany), while 53 percent of the CDU/CSU partisans tended to rank their party first and the SPD last (Noelle-Neumann, 1981:196). In such a context, where party rankings are so constrained by partisanship and ideological orientation, do party rankings also tend to covary with the perceived climate of opinion?

In the surveys I examined, respondents were asked the following two questions: "Do you think most people are pleased with the CDU/CSU?" and "Do you think most people are pleased with the SPD?" (Unfortunately, the question was not asked for the FDP.) Obviously, neither question alone is sufficient as a measure of the perceived climate of opinion for the population—respondents could easily answer "yes" or "no" to both questions, as the questions are not mutually exclusive for the two parties. I thus created a measure for the relative perceived popularity of the two parties by subtracting the percentage of respondents who said "most people" were pleased with the CDU/CSU from the percentage of respondents who said "most people" were pleased with the SPD. I also created a comparable scale for the rankings of the two parties by subtracting the percentage of respondents who ranked the CDU/CSU first from the percentage of respondents who ranked the SPD first in the preference orderings. I then graphed the results of these two measures for two time periods: October 1978 through October 1979, and January 1980 through January 1981. The first period contained results from 11 surveys of 2,000 persons each, while the second period contained results from 8 surveys of 2,000 persons each. The results are presented in Figures 11 and 12.

The graphs reveal a striking covariance between the relative perceived popularity of the two parties and the tendency of respondents to rank either of the two parties in first place. This relationship is especially pronounced for extreme changes; when a party experienced a marked increase or decrease in perceived support, respondents became more or less likely to rank that party first, respectively.

These results have several implications. First, changes in party rankings undoubtedly tend to be constrained by the individual's partisan and ideological orientations, both of which tend to be long-term commitments. Most changes are probably due primarily to the movement of people with a weak sense of partisanship and ideological commitment, who are more susceptible to the threat of isolation when a party's perceived popularity shifts. In this context, an individual's commitment to a particular party or ideology is a reflection of his "party differential"— or in terms from the preceding analysis, as a reflection of the value of C, or the cost of conforming to prevailing opinion, for the individual voter making the choice. Persons with low party differentials should tend to be more easily swayed by the perceived climate of opinion. Using the previous terms, it is more likely that in these cases, C', or the threat

Figure 11
Perception of the climate of opinion and party rankings

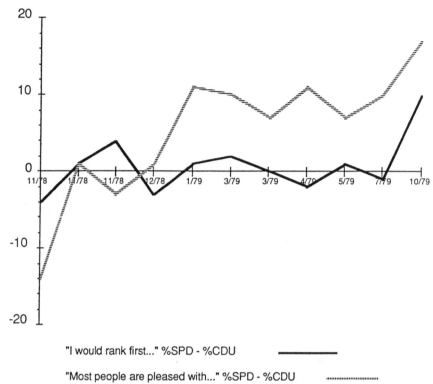

"I would rank first..." %SPD - %CDU   ─────────

"Most people are pleased with..." %SPD - %CDU   ································

Source: Allensbach Surveys 3060 (11/78), 3061 (10, 11/78) 3062 (11/78), 3063 (12/78), 3064 (1/
     '79), 3065 (3/79), 3066 (3/79), 3067 (4/79), 3070 (5/79), 3071 (7/79), 3074 (10/74).

of isolation, will exceed C, or the individual's party differential, for people willing to change their votes to conform to prevailing opinion. Hence, individuals with small or nonexistent party differentials are comparable to individuals who must contribute a small amount to collective action in order to avoid isolation. For just as contribution becomes more likely as C decreases, so should shifts in party preferences be more likely among persons with a lesser commitment to a given party.

This transition from party rankings to voting intentions has yet to be justified, however. To test whether voting intention covaried with the perceived climate of opinion, I used the same measure as before for the latter value, subtracting the percentage who felt "most people" were pleased with the CDU/CSU from the percentage who felt "most people" were pleased with the SPD. I then created a comparable measure for voting intention by subtracting the percentage of people intending to

Figure 12
Perception of the climate of opinion and party rankings

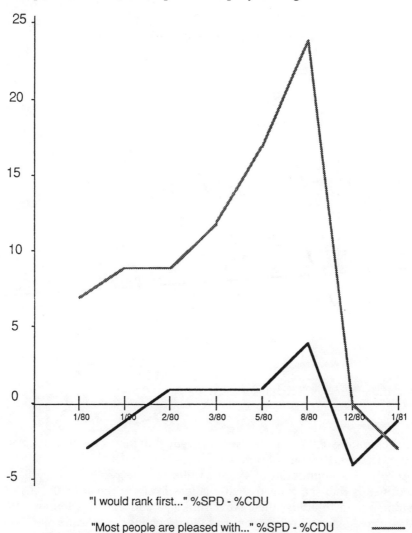

"I would rank first..." %SPD - %CDU ━━━━━

"Most people are pleased with..." %SPD - %CDU ▬▬▬▬

Source: Allensbach surveys 3077 (1/80), 3078 (1/80), 3079 (2/80), 3080 (3/80), 3082 (5/80), 3085 (8/80), 3091 (11, 12/80), 3092 (1/81)

vote for the CDU/CSU from the percentage of people intending to vote for the SPD. Six surveys of 2,000 persons each were included in this analysis; the surveys were fielded between December 1974 and March 1976. The graphic results of both measures, shown in Figure 13, are striking: voting intentions covaried almost exactly with the relative perceived climate of opinion regarding the two parties.[3] Voting intention,

Figure 13
Perception of the climate of opinion and voting intention

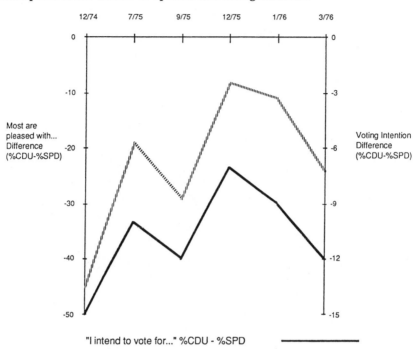

Source: Allensbach Jahrbuch, 1976; p. 132.

like the ranking of the political parties, seemed to follow the fluctuations in the perceived climate of opinion.

An obvious implication of these results for the problem of cyclical majorities is that the transitive rule is less likely to remain valid if individuals tend to adjust their party rankings and voting intentions to the perceived climate of opinion. But the problems of cyclical majorities and transitivity are not being directly addressed here. Instead, we are discussing whether people are likely to express an opinion contrary to the perceived dominant opinion concerning the two parties. If, in any given case, individuals tend to move toward the more popular position, it weakens the legitimacy of any claims contrary to that position based upon prior rules such as transitivity. Similarly, it limits the capacity of a less than decisive subset of the population to manipulate the outcome of a given choice system by voting for the less popular alternative—the method upon which strategic manipulation of voting depends (Barry and Hardin, 1982:14).

There are limits to any conclusions based upon these results, however. The best test of any resolution to the problem of cyclical majorities, whether in favor of the transitive rule or majority rule, would be to show how the proposed resolution alleviates this problem when it arises. According to the spiral of silence theory, however, the prior conditions for the voter's paradox—the advancement of a minority position based upon the transitive rule—imply their own solution because individuals in the minority tend to fall silent. The usefulness of this resolution may therefore not be tested. We are limited to examining the prior conditions for the voter's paradox and evaluating the likelihood of these conditions arising. Given the spiral of silence theorems and the preceding evidence, conflicts between the transitive and majority rules appear less likely than proponents of the problems suggest.

A final note is in order concerning these results. In chapter 4, I stated that the spiral of silence theory addressed the Arrow problem by making majority rule a privileged rule in social decisions. If this claim is valid, then the theory should also resolve the problem of cyclical majorities in a society. But we must take care to understand the structure of this argument. I do *not* argue that the fear of isolation necessarily "solves" the Arrow problem because it appears to resolve the voter's paradox in favor of majority rule. Cyclical preferences are but one specific, if evocative, counter example that illustrate the impossibility of satisfying Arrow's five conditions. Instead, I argue that because the spiral of silence theorems respond to the Arrow problem by questioning the validity of the transitive rule, this resolution should also carry over into the specific instances of this problem, including the case of cyclical majorities and the problem of collective action. The preliminary empirical evidence suggests that this response does appear valid for certain specific instances studied in this chapter. But no empirical analysis can "prove" the validity of an axiomatic assumption. We may only derive the expected effects that follow from the axiom and test whether these effects correspond to social behavior. The analysis of cyclical majorities was therefore postponed to a later part of this chapter to avoid the impression that a resolution of this problem necessarily implied a resolution of the general Arrow problem.

Of course, "resolving" the Arrow problem in favor of majority rule does not solve all the problems associated with invalidating the transitive rule, for by stating that transitivity is invalid, we deny our intuitive acceptance of the rule and the behavior it implies. Some behavioral implications of this assumption are explored in the final chapter, which discusses the qualitative effects of the resolution proposed here.

CONCLUSION

This chapter introduced a form of empirical analysis that many public choice theorists would claim is flawed at the outset. Barry, among others, admonished against adding such "non-economic" factors as altruism, guilt, and so on, into the equation of collective behavior on the individual level (Barry, 1978:14–15). But the analyses in this chapter approach the problem from a different perspective. These analyses concerned the aggregate level effects upon collective behavior that we would expect, given changes in the perceived or actual climate of opinion, and consistent costs over time. Is this analysis similarly prone to the criticisms advanced by collective choice theorists, or can we make the case that this approach allows us to address certain problems that the collective choice theorists must avoid? In order to answer this question, it is useful to review the criticisms that Hardin levels at "modified theories of collective action":

There is a growing literature on what is called a modified theory of collective action. The modified theory takes account of more variables in an individual's so-called expanded calculus of whether or not to contribute. Avoiding a feeling of guilt, cultivating a feeling of goodness, and numerous other variables are summed in as additional costs and benefits of contributing or not contributing to collective action. There are two strong objections to such an expanded calculus. First, the results are too flimsy to be worth the efforts, since most of the relevant behavior may be explained by the narrowest assessment of costs and benefits, and the host of motivations underlying the additional motivations is far more crudely measured than the narrowest cost-benefit motivations. Second, the focus of such theory is usually shifted from explaining the behavior of a particular group to explaining the behavior of those in the group who *do* join in cooperative enterprise, especially in an interest group organization, so that it is not the logic, but the problem, of collective action that has been modified. (Hardin, 1982:14)

Both of these objections relate to the empirical study of collective action situations outside of what Hardin calls the "narrowest cost-benefit analysis." My analysis in this chapter fits this description, albeit in a different manner than past analyses. It seems only fair, then, to evaluate the standard collective action model by Hardin's standards, to test whether it is more useful than the "expanded" approach described in this chapter.

Let us consider the second criticism first, for collective action theorists also tend to deal with a narrow range of cases in the evidence used to support their conclusions. Analyses of collective action do not usually observe a "latent group" and analyze why it does not become a "privileged group." Part of the reason is definitional—how does one identify a "latent group" within a population? One might speculate upon the preconditions for latency, such as the existence of a common interest and a shared awareness of that common interest. But in most analyses of collective action, this is not done. Instead, to paraphrase Hardin's criticism, collective action theorists usually refer to latent groups in the population (with little or no prior definition of why they are classified as latent) and then go on to study the existence and decline of privileged groups. There are obvious reasons why analysts prefer studying groups that exist. But the main topic of collective action theory—groups that do not exist—are discussed primarily with reference to the reader's intuition about groups that do or should exist in a society. Consider that Olson only spends two pages of his analysis discussing those "forgotten groups" that supposedly share interests but are latent, even while admitting that such groups are the major focus of his argument:

Unhappily, this is the type of group about which least is known, and about which very little can be said. The remaining type of group is the unorganized group—*the group that has no lobby and takes no action. Groups of this kind fit the main argument of this book best of all.* They illustrate its central point: that large or latent groups have no tendency to act voluntarily to further their common interests, ...for the unorganized groups, the groups that have no lobbies and exert no pressure, are among the largest groups in the nation, and they have some of the most vital common interests. (Olson, 1965:165; emphases mine)

Olson's examples of such latent groups illustrate one irony of this statement; the groups include migrant farm workers, taxpayers, and consumers, all of whom were to form important organizations soon after the publication of Olson's book. I do not single out these examples to criticize Olson's predictive abilities. Social scientists are remarkably poor predictors of future events, and one must admire Olson's candor for describing this gap in his analysis so explicitly. However, merely observing that a group appears to share a common interest is insufficient evidence to label that group as "latent." As a result, collective action studies focus upon the rise and decline of organized groups, despite Olson's claim that latent groups are the central topic of his study.

But what alternative exists for evaluating collective action? Let us note that latent groups are difficult to identify and study precisely because they are inactive—put in other terms, these groups are silent in terms of political speech and action. Indeed, these groups recall V. O. Key's notion of "latent opinion" as opinions that are in a "state of hibernation" and that are not expressed without the appropriate stimuli or support (Key, 1961:263–69). Furthermore, Key links his notion of latency to Truman's notion of "potential groups," described in *The Governmental Process* (Truman, 1952:33). But both Key's and Truman's notions return us to Noelle-Neumann's theory of public opinion, which deals as much with opinions (or behavior) that are silenced as with those that are expressed. Noelle-Neumann's theory gives us the framework by which we can observe groups that are latent or privileged within a society (or at some stage of development in between). The identification of these groups involves investigating whether a form of collective action was generally practiced at various times in the society, and then tracing the state of the action to the perceived and actual climate of opinion regarding this action (assuming costs of contribution remain constant). Implicit here is the notion that "latent" and "privileged" classifications are not absolute categories for describing groups in a society. Instead, latency tended to increase or decrease as public approval for collective action decreased or increased, respectively. The threat of isolation, as a force inherent in public opinion, seemed to transform the status of groups in a society.

But here we encounter the first, and related, objection that Hardin raises regarding alternative collective action analyses: Is it appropriate to "add" into the model a motivation like the fear of isolation, especially when we offer few additional measures of this motivation beyond the data on changes in the climate of opinion? A response must be framed with reference to my previous comments regarding expressed opinions or silence. For the fear of isolation is not a motivation that is "added into" the analysis of collective behavior; it is a motivation present in any form of such behavior. Its presence is not realized in most cases because the necessary preconditions for collective action—awareness of a common interest and a shared perception of that interest—are not met if approval for the action is not emerging as a dominant opinion in the society. We do not realize that silencing processes occur to discourage the organization and expression of viewpoints that we consider "latent."

Nowhere is this lack of recognition perhaps more evident than in Hardin's description of an "extrarational motivation" that encourages mass movements in a society—the "desire . . . to have oneself develop through participation in significant, even world-shaping historical events and movements" (Hardin, 1982:108). The author describes this motivation in several ways: as a "motivation which some would class as narrowly self-interested and some as moral," as "the desire to be there, *to take part in history*," and as the wish described by Tolstoy "*to share the experiences of [an individual's] time and place*" (Hardin, 1982:108–109; emphases mine). Hardin attributes to this motivation activities as sweeping as participation in the civil rights and women's movements, and as commonplace as voting (Hardin, 1982:111–12). His description has a strong intuitive appeal; we are aware of the feelings he describes. But his description is also incomplete, for it begs the following question: How do we know which actions are appropriate, at any given time and place, to "participate in our history"? The only reasonable response is that we obtain this knowledge in the same way that we obtain knowledge about changing fashions—by observing our social environment. Such participation thus implies conformity, in statement or speech, to the emerging or prevailing consensus of public opinion one observes about current issues and the political agenda. This fact of political and social life so often makes the motivations of one political generation incomprehensible to preceding or subsequent generations. This condition also catches past analysts unaware when new social movements emerge. The source of this consensus may be impossible to trace. Most analyses of social movements tend to be after the fact, focusing upon social conditions rather than the sources of awareness about these conditions. Yet, the key element in these analysis remains the awareness of shared opinions that transforms potential movements into actual movements.

We may therefore trace Hardin's motivation to "participate in one's history" to the same public opinion processes underlying fashion, conformity to social conventions, and other forms of collective behavior. Consider Noelle-Neumann's general statement regarding the motivations behind these actions:

Anyone looking carefully will find, underlying them all, that layer Locke called the unwritten law of opinion, or reputation, or fashion. We find everywhere the strict pattern that, for Locke, justifies using the term "law": *Rewards and punishments following not from the act itself . . . but from approval or disapproval given by the social environment at a certain time and in a certain place.* (Noelle-Neumann, 1984:118; emphases mine)

Public opinion carries with it its own sense of time and place and this sense defines the actions necessary to "participate in one's history." Such participation may involve Hardin's examples of "going to war, or not going to war" (Hardin, 1981:112), or Noelle-Neumann's example of choosing to wear a beard in a particular era (Noelle-Neumann, 1984:116). But this realization implies a conclusion that Hardin does not reach: *we are always participating in our history,* insofar as "our history" refers to a collective political and social experience that we share with others during a particular time in a society. Participation in history is not like a water tap that we turn on or off depending upon our mood. It is an ongoing, constant process of conformity to the prevailing or emerging consensus, to which we pay tribute by expressing certain opinions and behavior and silencing others. Of course, not all people conform to this consensus at all times (recall the discussion of exchange curves between C and C'). However, such conformity is a general tendency of individuals existing in a society. Silence or inactivity is thus a response, a form of "participation in history," that we tend to ignore in analyses that focus upon activity and expression. Yet, our intuitive understanding of this response underlies our notion of "latent" groups or opinions in a society.

A final note regarding Olson's analysis and this interpretation of collective behavior is necessary. The fear of isolation, as it is described here, is not a "selective incentive" that rewards individuals who contribute to collective action approved by the majority. Instead, the threat of isolation challenges the assumptions upon which the Arrow problem, and hence the problem of collective action, are founded from a different perspective than past challenges. As such, the spiral of silence theory prompts a reconsideration of Arrow's "reasonable conditions," and a re-evaluation of the specific examples represented by cyclical group preferences, the Prisoners' dilemma, and the problem of collective action. Some empirical implications of this re-evaluation have been explored in the preceding pages. In the final chapter I will explore some qualitative implications of the restructuring of these problems, by focusing upon systems that embrace majority rule as a privileged rule, for Noelle-Neumann's analysis allows us to redefine the notion of "social preference" in a manner that avoids Mackie's "fallacy of composition." This redefined notion has profound qualitative effects upon the way we perceive social interactions and collective decision making.

NOTES

1. Hardin argues in his chapter on "Extrarational Motivations" in *Collective Action* that females might have joined the women's movement because "consciousness raising" could have been a selective benefit for contributors (Hardin, 1982:33). This seems to me an odd argument; "consciousness raising" does not seem to be an end in itself, but rather a means to the end of forming some kind of solidarity with other women to advance their mutual interests. As such, one does not join in collective action to participate in consciousness raising; one participates in consciousness raising as a preliminary step toward collective action.

2. Unless otherwise indicated, all of the data for these analyses are drawn from the archives at the Institut für Demoskopie Allensbach, which has some of the best information concerning changes in the climate of opinion and the perceived climate of opinion on collective action over time.

3. Note that I am not claiming that all problems that Arrow and others associate with cyclical group preferences will be solved by invalidating the transitive rule. It will still be impossible under these circumstances to reach a decision that meets Arrow's five conditions. I will explore the implications of this result in the final chapter.

7

The Redefined Notion of "Social Preference"

The preceding discussions of Arrow's theorem have introduced some reservations about his use of the notion "social preference," particularly with reference to his demand for transitivity in the definition of a social welfare function (SWF). Plott (1982:243) and Barry and Hardin (1982:376) also express reservations about this usage, albeit from a different perspective than the one outlined here. These authors advocate abandoning the notion as an example of the fallacy of composition. I would disagree with this strategy, for even though the notion of "social preference" is misused in much of the social choice literature, it is more useful to redefine rather than abandon the idea. Barry and Hardin's criticisms do provide a useful departure point for a redefinition, however. They argue that social preference is nothing more than a "metaphor drawn from individual experience and extended incautiously beyond the sphere in which it has a well-defined sense" (Barry and Hardin, 1982:376).

The notion of "social preference" as a metaphor extended inappropriately from individual preferences to group decisions should be discarded. Indeed, I made this point in chapter 4, when I rejected the transitive rule. However, I also advanced an alternative explanation of why we expected social decisions to be transitive. This expectation rested upon an inadequate understanding of the public opinion processes that make social choices appear unanimous or nearly unanimous once they are decided. This alternative explanation commits us to an alternative definition of the notion of social preference.

Let us first consider a few of the various ways in which a preference for x over y may be expressed and interpreted by the society's members. Barry and Hardin state that the appropriate statement of a decision process's outcome is "x is preferred to y." Plott goes further, endowing this statement with a stronger qualitative element: because "x is preferred to y," we may assume that the society has decided "x is better than y" (Plott, 1982:238). However, the spiral of silence theory implies an expression and interpretation of this social preference that differs from either of these statements, for when the preference of x over y is emerging as the dominant opinion, the appropriate statement is "x is the social preference and y is not," according to the theorems described in chapter 2. Furthermore, this statement implies that x is set equivalent to the social preference out of the choice set $[x,y]$, while y is silenced as a preference in the society. In the redefined notion of "social preference," the society prefers x to y when the statement "x is the social preference and y is not" is the dominant opinion, and the statement "y is the social preference" is generally silenced.

These statements are quite different in content from Plott's and Barry and Hardin's statements, given the use of language they imply and the conventions of language they define for the times during which they hold sway in a society. Recall Barry's statement in *Political Argument* that "Communication by means of language is only possible if there are *conventions prescribing the normal intentions that those using the words must share*" (Barry, 1965:10; emphases mine). One result of a public opinion process that defines x as the social preference, then, is the creation of a convention of language unique to the time and circumstances under which it is generated. Beyond its appropriate context, the statement "x is the social preference" may become invalid, or incomprehensible. To extend this statement beyond its appropriate context would be invalid and could possibly lead to errors in the calculation of social decisions. Noelle-Neumann describes the nature and limits of conventions of language and commonly accepted definitions that grow out of the public opinion process:

We must come to grips with this reality of public opinion, *this creation that is tied to a space, tied to a time*. Otherwise, we shall deceive ourselves into supposing that we would not have kept quiet when the emperor entered in his new clothes. The Andersen fairy tale is about public opinion dominating a scene, reigning at a particular place. If a stranger had happened to enter, he could scarcely have contained his surprise.

And there is the matter of time. As those who have come later, we shall judge as unjustly and as ignorantly as people in the Middle Ages judged on the causes of sickness. *We shall make judgments about words and actions of the past as if they had spoken or occurred in our times, but, in doing so, we shall become ignoramuses who know nothing about the fervor of an age*. . . . That is the Zeitgeist boiled down to a formula, as Lippmann described it. He also described how, later, formulas crumble and then become incomprehensible to those who follow.

To sharpen one's feelings for the times, and simultaneously, one's understanding of public opinion would be a goal worth reaching and training for. What does it mean to be a "contemporary"? What does "timelessness" mean? Why did Hegel urgently point to the element of time: "He who is able to express what his times are saying and to carry out what they want is the great man of the time"? (Noelle-Neumann, 1984:180–81; emphases mine)

This element of time in public opinion and preference expression will be explored presently, for its implications for the use and interpretation of social preference are profound. First, however, let us examine the convention of language generated by majority choices between paired alternatives, assuming our redefined notion of social preference. Here, too, the element of time is important. The classic case of cyclical majorities concerns three social decisions made at three different times, concerning three sets of alternatives $[x,y]$, $[y,z]$, and $[w,z]$, for if we were using majority rule to decide among rankings in the three-choice set, no ranking of the three alternatives could become the social preference.

Hence, let us deal with the choice set of $[x,y]$ at $t = t_1$, $[y,z]$ at $t = t_2$, and $[x,z]$ at $t = t_3$. Let us assume, in keeping with the classic case of cyclical preferences that at $t = t_1$, "x is the social preference and y is not." Similarly, at $t = t_2$, "y is the social preference and z is not," and at $t = t_3$, "z is the social preference and x is not." According to Noelle-Neumann's description of public opinion, we have defined three different conventions of language (and most probably, of behavior). These conventions are peculiar to the place or context (which is described by the alternatives presented) and the time (e.g. t_1, t_2, t_3) in which they were generated. More importantly, these conventions only hold for the place (or context) and time in which they were created. We witness the breakdown of the logic behind the transitive rule, which demands that social preferences be defined as xPy and yPz at different times and that these statements remain true outside of the time in which they were created. According to the theory of public opinion, and the redefinition of social preference which it implies, both assumptions need not necessarily be valid.

There is another way of considering this conclusion. A good part of the social choice literature has been devoted to arguing whether individual or social preferences should be considered cardinal or ordinal, as this decision affects the manner in which we perceive social choices (see the brief discussion of additive utilitarianism and the "new welfare economics" in Barry and Hardin, 1982:213–14). When one deals with pairs of alternatives, this distinction is moot; any dichotomy may be considered nominal, ordinal, or cardinal in measurement, and all paired choices, when taken alone, may be interpreted as dichotomies. When one moves beyond two alternatives, however, this distinction becomes highly relevant. At what level is the "preference" for one state of affairs over another measured in the redefined notion of social preference? In the above example, we describe a social convention in which x is "named" the social preference at $t = t_1$, y is "named" the social preference at $t = t_2$, and z is "named" the social preference at $t = t_3$. The "social preference" for one state of affairs over another becomes nominal, and the restrictions that apply to the conclusions one may reach with nominal level measures apply in a similar manner here. This conclusion is important, for the transitive rule does not work with nominal level choices—only with ordinal or cardinal level choices. Hence, much of the confusion concerning majority rule occurs because analysts interpret a majority decision as an ordinal or cardinal value.

How disruptive is the redefinition of social preference as a nominal convention of language resulting from the public opinion process? One may test whether the redefinition is acceptable, given our common experiences with social behavior and collective decision making, by applying it to examples of cyclical preferences and the problem of collective action. I will concentrate first on the issue of cyclical group preferences and fashion and then turn to the problem of collective action. I will also discuss the role of time in both problems, as it is affected by the redefined notion of social preference.

FASHION, TIME, AND SOCIAL PREFERENCE

At the outset of this discussion, one must distinguish between social decisions that occur in a relatively open context, in which conventions of language are fluid and open to definition, and social decisions that occur in a relatively closed context, in which conventions of language regarding decision making are already established (and may be set down in formal rules). I categorize consumer choices in the market and public opinion in the former category, and institutional decisions in the latter category (even when those institutions derive their authority from their constituents' choice of representatives). This distinction differs somewhat from Schotter's approach, as he classifies the market as but one institution among many in which social decisions may occur (Schotter, 1981:8). But social decisions in the context of the creation of conventions of language require a different distinction. Established institutions carry with them their own conventions of language that one must accept in order to operate within them. Although these conventions may change (usually heralding a change in the institution as well), each social decision does not imply as great a potential for changing the discourse of decision making as may occur in the noninstitutional context. I discuss decision making in relatively open context in this section, and reserve the discussion of decision making in more restrictive institutional contexts for a later section.

What effects might a nominal definition of "social preference" have upon our understanding of social decisions in a relatively open context? First, this redefinition alters the equation of "rationality" with the transitive rule, even as that rationality is reflected in individual-level decisions to accept or reject transitivity in expressed preferences. It is useful here to proceed by example, by examining the problems that arise when the cardinal notion of social preference is used. Barry and Hardin provide two examples where these problems occur, defining two difficulties with the intransitivity of expressed individual preferences: problems of communication and problems of personal choice.

Consider the problems of communication described in the following example:

If I contradict myself—in the simplest instance, assert A and not A—*I have not succeeded in communicating anything.* Now consider a more complex type of inconsistency. If I say John is taller than Mary, Mary is taller than Joe, and Joe is taller than John, *I have not produced a coherent statement about the relative heights of John, Mary, or Joe. There is no way of fitting my assertions together so as to come up with a consistent ordering of the three in terms of height.* Similarly, if I say I prefer apples to pears, pears to bananas, and bananas to apples, *I have not expressed a coherent preference ordering among the three kinds of fruit.* Depending upon where I stop in the cycle of preferences I have set up, I can put any of them at the top of my list. Note that I am not saying that they are equally good. Rather, I am saying that each is better than the others—which is absurd. . . . When such inconsistencies are pointed out, we should, *if we are rational,* admit that something is wrong and be prepared to bring our previous judgments into consistency with one another. (Barry and Hardin, 1982:371; emphases mine)

Initially, these examples seem somewhat limited in their application to the redefined notion of social preference. In the first case, for instance, we are dealing with an implied standard measure (i.e. height, measured in whatever units are used) where the comparisons are indisputably cardinal. But the authors' arguments about communication and rationality are useful, for they raise two questions regarding rationality and transitivity: May an individual express seemingly intransitive preferences in social decisions in a manner that does communicate something and may this expression be interpreted as "rational" under the right conditions?

The authors reply negatively to the second question, in a manner that provides a useful departure point for discussing both issues:

It is sometimes suggested that rationality, understood in this sense, is a value that someone may or may not accept. We have no business, it is claimed, criticizing people if they choose not to act according to its precepts. However, a failure to reconcile one's pairwise preferences into a single ordering may, to put the matter at the crassest possible level, be expensive. Suppose that you prefer a Rabbit to a full-size Chevrolet because it costs about the same and is more economical on fuel; and that you prefer a BMW to a Rabbit because it is fuel efficient and a good deal roomier; and that you prefer a Chevrolet to a BMW because it is even more roomy, costs a lot less, and spare parts for it are cheaper and easier to come by. You could lose an awful lot of money to get back to where you began if you acted on your pairwise preferences—and unless you realized what was happening, there would be nothing (except bankruptcy) to prevent you from going around the cycle again and again. To put the point formally, if you prefer A to B, B to C, and C to A, this should imply (otherwise what does it mean) that you would be willing to give up something (i.e., money) to get from A to B, from B to C, and from C to A, and so on, indefinitely. Thus, *your cyclic preferences could be a source of continuous income to a sharp entrepreneur. The connections between rationality and elementary prudence in the conduct of one's affairs thus looks compelling.* (Barry and Hardin, 1982:371–72; emphases mine)

Let us consider my above questions in an example similar to the one presented by the authors. Recalling the discussion of fashion, rationality, and conformity in chapter 5, let us describe the hypothetical tastes and consumer preferences of people buying dress shirts. In a given season, the fashion might tend toward wide collared, brightly colored shirts (which a majority prefers to narrow collared white shirts). The individual conforms to fashion and purchases the former style. In the next season, the fashion tends toward buttoned down, colored shirts (which a majority prefers to the wide collared variety). The individual also conforms to this fashion by purchasing the new style shirt and consigning the past season's shirts to the back of his closet. In the next season, the fashion tends toward narrow collared, white shirts (which a majority prefers to the buttoned down, colored shirts). Once again, the individual buys new shirts to conform to style, consigning the past season's shirts to the back of his closet.

In these three sets of paired choices, the consumer has expressed a cyclical preference in his buying patterns. He preferred wide collared colored shirts to narrow collared white shirts, buttoned down colored shirts to wide collared colored shirts, and narrow collared white shirts to buttoned down colored shirts across the three seasons. Has this consumer (and others like him) "failed to communicate anything" by displaying intransitive preferences in behavior? By conforming to fashion at each step in purchases, he has communicated something—a desire to stay in fashion for the time and choices with which he was presented. He is, to use Hardin's terms, "participating in his own history" by communicating his conformity to the conventions of proper dress, however mundane this conformity may appear. But this merely restates the point that participation in one's history is an ongoing process of conformity to the present or emerging consensus, directed toward avoiding isolation, even at considerable cost to the actor. Conventions of behavior and dress are statements that are coherent in this case, but only in the nominal sense of participating in the definition of a convention, or a "social preference." The transitive rule for communicating preferences is inoperable in this instance. The individual's choices are coherent for the times in which he made them, and only coherent for those times.

Now let us consider the second question: is the individual "irrational" in his behavior? Conceding that conformity to fashion may be quite expensive (given the price of dress shirts), we also understand that the individual makes a trade off between the cost of the item and the threat of isolation when he purchases items in the new fashion. This behavior is not irrational; it defines a motivation common in the marketplace and in other forms of social interactions where new conventions of expression may be created. The irony is that these conclusions hold even if we accept most of the conditions Barry and Hardin describe. Changes in fashion—be they in dress, cars, or political behavior—are a source of continuous income (or power) to "sharp entrepreneurs" who can successfully anticipate and exploit these changes. There is nothing mysterious occurring here. In fact, designers would readily admit that it is by successful anticipation of fashion trends that they remain in business.[1]

The dynamics of public opinion and silencing that I have described apply to all forms of social behavior. However, proponents of the transitive rule might understandably cry foul at this point. They could argue that the time during which the consumer's choices occurred was simply too long for us to expect reasonably that the transitive rule would apply. There are two problems with this argument. First, there is no explicit time limit on the validity of the transitive rule, assuming that other conditions (i.e. individuals' tastes and the decision-making rules) remain constant. Second, the transitive rule's structure implies a timespan between the accumulation of results to which the principle is applied. The transitive rule is expressly designed to link together information about preferences gathered at different times (however far apart), and out of different choice pairs.

Let us consider the former response first. While there is no explicit time limit for applying the transitive rule (assuming preferences remain constant), there could be an *implicit* expectation that the rule will be applied to choices made within a reasonable time limit. But then how do we empirically define a "reasonable" time limit for the validity of the rule? Furthermore, should we establish a rule as an axiomatic principle if that rule's validity begins to deteriorate as the time between decisions increases?[2]

The second response carries this argument even further. One establishes the transitive rule as a condition specifically to link together decisions made at different times, and from different choice sets, into a final preference ordering. The manner in which we structure the decision process here assumes that the meaning of each decision will remain constant beyond the time and choice context in which it is made. But this assumption is purely a result of the way in which we structure and conceptualize the decision process. The above example with dress shirts shows how this assumption might not be valid if social preferences are considered nominal level conventions peculiar to their time and context. The relevant question, then, is whether the transitive condition is forced upon us by circumstances of political and social behavior. In consumer behavior, transitivity might not be a useful condition for describing "rational" decision-making behavior. Are there other decision-making situations in which we may reasonably abandon this choice structure, justified by the spiral of silence theorems? Our conclusions should also apply to the Prisoners' dilemma and the logic of collective action, as specific instances of Arrow's problem.

THE PRISONERS' DILEMMA, COLLECTIVE ACTION, AND SOCIAL PREFERENCE

Let us begin with the questions regarding rationality and communication that guided the previous analysis: can public opinion, as a process, restructure the logic in time of collective action, so that cooperation becomes a rational strategy? If so, does the individual who cooperates communicate something coherent about his ranking of preferred outcomes? In fact, discussions of the role of time in Prisoners' dilemma games are quite common in the literature. These discussions tend to approach the issue from a different perspective than the one we will use, but the past work provides a good departure point for analysis. Duncan Snidal provides a summary of the conditions under which time might be expected to have a positive effect upon the outcome of Prisoners' dilemma (PD) games:

It is widely understood that the prospect of repeated play into the future increases the likelihood of cooperation in PD even in the absence of centralized enforcement (Axelrod, 1984; Hardin, 1982; Shubik, 1970; Taylor, 1976). Although non-cooperation is a rational strategy in single-play PD, repeated play of the game into the future makes it worthwhile to take a chance on cooperating today in the hope that other states will do likewise and mutual cooperation will prevail over the deficient non-cooperation in the longer term. This possibility is more likely: (1) the longer the time horizon (or expected number of iterations of the game), since, as the final game approaches the incentive to cooperate because of future considerations diminishes; (2) the lower the temporal discount, or, equivalently, the more future benefits from cooperation are valued relative to the prevailing consensus not to cooperate; and (3) the greater the benefits from cooperation relative to the gains to be had from not cooperating (or the losses to be incurred from cooperating while other states do not). To the extent that these conditions are fulfilled, *the fact that a PD issue is recurring through time will facilitate cooperative behavior.* (Snidal, 1985:930–31)

At issue here are the conditions under which cooperation may be considered a "rational strategy," considering the time through which the PD game is played. The effect of time, according to Snidal and others, is that it may rearrange the preference orderings of outcomes for individuals if the game is repeated enough. However, Snidal does not address the issue of the time through which a single PD game is played, and as a result the structure imposed on the game (or any collective action situation). Consider how Snidal conceptualizes time for a single PD game:

If we treat "present" time as the duration of a single PD game embedded within an ongoing issue area, it becomes apparent that the speed with which states can adjust their policies (i.e. the duration of any single PD) has an impact similar to that of a longer time horizon. The faster that states adapt to each others' actions, the more iterations of the game there are in any fixed length of time. (Snidal, 1985:931; emphases mine)

The choice of an outcome in the PD game (out of the possibilities of z, x, y, and w described in chapter 3), occurs in the "present" time, according to Snidal's formulation. But what does the "present time" mean here? Obviously, the game is played out in "real time," so that the author is not implying that the outcome emerges instantaneously (in the "now," so to speak) for this game. Instead, the "present" obviously refers to a condition under which all relevant elements of the game—for example, the actors' preference orderings, the choices presented to them, and the manner of deciding among choices—do not change. But this definition requires a leap of faith justified by the transitive rule. Since transitivity is a necessary part of the PD problem, we allow this rule to take choices, which might be separate in time, and "pull" them into an artificial "present." The structure of the decision process and the manner in which choices are presented to actors affects the definition of "present" time in the PD game.

Must we necessarily accept this structure for the game? One might easily conceive of a PD game in which the outcomes are considered in discrete pairs that must be accepted unanimously, as described in chapter 3. In this case, only one pair of outcomes describes a convention of language that all may accept: "all cooperate" is the social preference, while "all defect" is not. All other outcomes would be vetoed by the individual(s) unwilling to cooperate while others defect. Here, we dis-

aggregate the "single" PD game into several games, in which each discrete pair of alternatives (i.e. [x,y], [x,z], [w,x], [w,y], [w,z]) would be
selected or rejected, each within its own "present" time (since time is
defined by the structure of the decision process). We thus come to two
critical questions regarding the PD game and its structure in time: Why
does Snidal consider that the choice among the full range of outcomes
must occur in "present" time and may the PD game be restructured in
time by the redefined notion of social preference, so that choices are
disaggregated into pairs in a useful manner?

Snidal's assumption derives from the implicit presence of the transitive
rule in this game and the problem of collective action. Transitivity demands that discrete outcomes reached, or collected, at different times
be linked together into an overall ordering. As such, the various elements
in the game (i.e. the choices offered and the preference orderings) are
considered "simultaneously" (i.e. in the "present" time), in order that
they may be combined by this rule. But the transitive rule also provided
the final link between the Prisoners' dilemma problem and the Arrow
problem by generating two contradictory outcomes: one where players
preferred cooperation to defection (in paired choices) and one where
players were indifferent between these alternatives (in the combined,
transitive social ordering).

If we could invalidate the transitive rule in favor of a series of discrete
decisions between paired alternatives (with each decision played out in
its own "present" time), the structure and outcome of the game could
change. This restructuring, which was reasonable in the case of cyclical
majorities, is similarly reasonable for the PD problem.

Let us recall the purest theoretical case of collective action problems
outlined in chapter 5. Within the two-dimensional Individual/Collective
matrix, each individual is faced with a unanimous opinion that he should
contribute to the collective good. He must balance his social utility of
contributing to avoid isolation with his social utility of not contributing
to avoid the cost of paying. All individuals find themselves in a situation
similar to the consumer in my previous example in PD games involving
more than two persons. If all persons pay in order to avoid isolation,
the game is reduced to two outcomes, "all contribute" or "all defect,"
with the former outcome being chosen (assuming approval is the dominant opinion). The other outcomes are not even considered. A situation
arises similar to the one where paired alternatives are considered separately, and the other outcomes are shown to be unworkable. The threat
of isolation restructures the problem by bringing forward this choice of
outcomes worked out in "present" time, while eliminating all other
possibilities. The "individual" is "rational" insofar as he chooses to
pursue his social utility at the expense of his individual ability. He com-

municates a desire to conform to the prevailing consensus regarding collective action.

It is now necessary to complicate the model. For we know that in most (if not all) real life situations, costs for collective goods are not symmetrically distributed among all members of a society. Indeed, in the Prisoners' dilemma problem I have described, the unanimous rule need not limit the possible outcomes to "all cooperate" or "all defect" in games with more than two people. Since the majority can always (in theory) coerce the minority to pay by threatening social isolation, any outcome is possible where the minority pays and the majority does not, since the majority would approve of such an outcome. Also, there are institutional procedures that make use of the transitive rule in reaching decisions, in violation of the nondictatorship axiom in Arrow's proof.[3] Are these instances where the three theorems do not hold sway? If so, how can we claim that these institutions are supported by democratic procedures if they are not affected by the forces that make majority rule privileged? Can the redefined notion of social preference explain the existence of asymmetric costs and benefits, and the uneven distribution of institutional power?

These questions may be addressed, if one considers the other factors in the model. These factors include the different sensitivities individuals or groups have to the threat of isolation, and the different costs that can result from the distribution of these sensitivities in the population. These factors define conditions under which individuals will accept a structure for decision making other than the one I have described here. The discussion of these conditions requires two steps: we must understand why we generally expect social costs to be "equitably" distributed in a society and we must discover why gross inequalities in social costs may still result, despite our expectations.

ASYMMETRIES IN COLLECTIVE DECISION MAKING

Why does an "equal" distribution of social costs for collective goals appear to be a "fair" and workable formula for assessing contributions? The discussion of collective action in chapters 5 and 6 assumed that the costs of contributing to a collective goal or activity were equal for all persons who chose to do so. This assumption follows Hardin's example from chapters 2 through 4 in *Collective Action*; he states that "all members have identical interest in the collective good: all place the same value on a given unit of the collective good supplied, and all place the same value on a unit of cost" (Hardin, 1982:67). My analysis did include the value of avoiding isolation, C', and I acknowledged that C' could have different values for different individuals. Still, I assumed that A_i and C

remain constant for all members of society. My empirical analysis studied the behavior of individuals in a given society when the costs and benefits of collective action remained constant over time, but where the value of C', measured by the perceived and actual climate of opinion, varied. Even the discussion of exchange curves between C and C', which introduced more variance into the analysis, still defined a fairly restrictive model, given the constant values of A_i and C.

What are the possibilities that a differential distribution of costs and benefits could occur in this model? To begin the discussion simply, assume that individuals will always exchange a given cost C to avoid the threat of isolation from not contributing to a popular collective goal. Put aside momentarily any discussion of exchange curves between C and C'. But let us make this assumption only if the value of C is the same for all individuals in the society—that is, if costs of collective action are equally distributed.

What will occur if costs and benefits are suddenly *not* equally distributed in the population? If the total cost of collective action in a society has the value of C_t, then it may be distributed among the society's members in any possible combination. If the majority has the capacity to coerce the minority to contribute to collective action through the threat of isolation, it is unlikely that costs and benefits will be equally distributed among all members of the population. Instead, it is more likely that a majority of a given size will force a minority to pay all costs of supporting the action, while the majority accrues all benefits (if possible) for itself.[4] Of course, moral and practical imperatives may prevent the majority from acting in this manner; however, we must acknowledge two points. First, self-interested individuals in the majority should be expected to act in this manner if they have the opportunity to do so. Second, there is nothing in the spiral of silence theory, as described so far in this section, that would prevent the majority from acting in this manner.[5]

This problem is not only a function of the spiral of silence theory with its implied threat of isolation; it may arise anytime a group of individuals has the ability to coerce others to comply with their decisions. Hardin's solution in his germinal article on collective action falls prey to this same difficulty. Hardin argues in a closing statement that "the existence of a Condorcet choice, which is by definition unique, implies that a real world group decide in favor of the Condorcet choice over every other *realizable* outcome. Consequently, it is rational in a world in which distrust seems endemic to use sanctions to force all members of an interest group to contribute towards the purchase of the group interest" (Hardin, 1971:479; emphases mine). Hardin begins with the set of "realizable outcomes" and then introduces the possibility of sanctions or coercion. But sanctions or coercion alter the set of "realizable outcomes," by begging the question of what proportion of the group must approve of coercion to make those options viable. If any proportion of the group less than the total may approve and use coercion to force other members to contribute, then dissenters may be forced to pay the entire cost of collective action approved by the decisive (and controlling) subgroup as a "realizable outcome." Any responsive rule short of unanimity expands the range of possible outcomes and opens the door to unequal distributions of social costs, as long as the decisive subgroup controls the coercive apparatus. We return to a version of the problem raised in chapter 4 regarding whether democracy could become a privileged rule in society. If coercion can be used to force members to contribute anything to collective action (including their "fair share"), then why would a majority (or some other decisive subset of the group) not use coercion to make the minority bear all the costs of collective action? Conversely, if unanimous approval is needed to force everyone to pay their "fair share," as Hardin assumes, how would it operate—who would approve forcing themselves to do what they would not do otherwise? Finally, even if unanimous approval for coercion were a useful device given human nature, we have destroyed the distinction between public and private domains, and the spirit of "public choice."

Let us respond to these issues by appealing to experience. States governed by responsive rules do not require full approval by all citizens in order to be able to create social policy or assess citizens for social costs. Furthermore, such states usually make and defend their decisions regarding allocations of costs and benefits with reference to some standard of "fairness" or "equity." Why do they refer to such standards if the majority can coerce obedience through the threat of isolation? Do these standards have any meaning, or does the majority simply define them as a convention of language to justify their decisions? The answer lies in factors excluded from the model thus far in this section—the varying sensitivities different individuals have to the threat of isolation, and the distribution of exchange curves between C and C' that result.

THE DISTRIBUTION OF SOCIAL COSTS

The exchanges individuals make between the cost of contributing to a collective goal and the avoidance of isolation depend upon three factors: the strength of the threat of isolation (i.e. the value of C'), the costs involved (i.e. the value of C), and the sensitivity of individuals to the threat of isolation (which describes the shape of their exchange curves). Because exchange curves are assumed to be randomly distributed in the space defined by given values of C and C', the chances that an individual's curve will fall under a value of C' (so that he will pay the cost of avoiding isolation) decreases as the value of C increases. Hence, if the least decisive subset—here, the smallest possible majority—attempts to force the minority to pay all costs for a collective good, it lowers the chances that the threat of isolation will be sufficient to coerce payment from all or most individuals. A few members of the minority, who are especially sensitive to the threat of isolation, may be coerced into paying. But the good will probably not be provided, or will be provided at suboptimal levels because of insufficient contribution. Under these conditions the threat of isolation could be too weak, or the costs too high, to compel members of the minority to exchange C for C'. It is not definite that the good will not be provided, but the chances of provision are severely diminished.

How might this problem be addressed? The most obvious strategy is to lower the value of C for members of the minority. But since the total cost of the collective good C_t is fixed, the individual cost C may only be lowered by compelling more individuals in the society to bear some of the cost for the collective goal. As the cost of C decreases, the proportion of individuals willing to approve payment will increase, thereby increasing the threat of isolation for noncontributors. But even the increased value of C' might be insufficient to coerce noncontributors to pay if the cost C is still quite high. Once again, the majority risks losing provision of the collective good or having it supplied at suboptimal levels. The cost of contribution might therefore be lowered again, compelling more individuals to pay. If this process of adjustment can continue, one should reach a distribution of costs and benefits that guarantees that the collective goal will be reached—that is an "equitable" or "fair" distribution of costs among all group members. If the society is perceived as dropping below the equitable or fair distribution, provision of the collective good is once again endangered.

One is thus led to a rather startling conclusion regarding democratic systems, where majority rule is a privileged rule: *Such systems embrace "fairness" or "equity" as a goal not because they are prerequisites for the system, but because these standards are the most efficient for distributing social costs to insure maximum compliance with group decisions.* The system does not embrace fairness and equity because it is democratic; rather, it remains democratic because it embraces fairness and equity. As a preliminary conclusion, democratic societies remain stable by equating fairness and equity in the distribution of social costs.

THE LIMITS OF EQUITY

We must now face the second question raised regarding the distribution of social costs. Societies routinely declare their assessment of social costs to be "fair" but it is rare that their assessment is clearly equitable. "Fairness" and "equity" are rather slippery standards as distributive principles, open to a variety of interpretations. The two terms need not even be equivalent; in a given situation "fairness" could imply a different distribution of costs than "equity." Some of the problems of using "fairness" as a distributive principle are described in Barry's critique of Rawls. Here, Barry raises several problems with Rawls's a priori definition of fairness as an axiomatic principle for decision making:

In *A Theory of Justice*, the question of "stability" of a just society occupies a large place: to the extent that Part Three could be said to have a theme, this is it.

A society is "stable," in the relevant sense here, if there are *appropriate motives in human nature . . . to enable people to live up to the publicly recognized standards of justice without a great deal of coercion.* Rawls argues, for example, that the utilitarian principle is not compatible with stability because maximizing average utility may conceivably require that some be made wretched in order to make others happy indeed (see pages 175–78).

The criterion of potential stability therefore sets limits on the range of principles that can be chosen by the parties in the original position. "They cannot enter into agreements that may have consequences they cannot accept. They will avoid those that they can adhere to only with great difficulty," (page 176). Unfortunately, this argument is so powerful that it seems to be in imminent danger of short-circuiting the whole elaborate argument in favor of the "two principles [of fairness]." For if (as Rawls sometimes appears to imply) they are the only principles capable of satisfying the demands of stability, that would seem to end the matter then and there. In order to avoid this premature closure of the discussion, I shall, therefore, assume that the requirements of stability are compatible with a fairly wide range of possible principles. (Barry, 1973:14–15; emphases mine)

It is beyond my purposes here to review or critique Rawls's argument, particularly since I am not concerned with discussing alternative theories of justice. However, the twin notions of "stability" and "fairness," and the problems of linking the two, are germane to my discussion. I have argued that distributing social costs according to some standard of fairness as equity provides the most hospitable context for social choice to occur. If social costs are distributed fairly by this definition, then it is likely that the threat of isolation will have its greatest effect, "as an appropriate motive in human nature," to bring dissenting members to follow the will of the majority. However, the range of possible definitions of fairness makes the "requirements of stability . . . compatible with a fairly wide range of possible principles" in democratic societies. For notions of fairness, particularly regarding the distribution of social costs, seem particularly open to the vicissitudes of public opinion. To take but one example, it was generally accepted as fair, according to public consensus in the United States, that the nation should have a progressive income tax system for collecting revenues. Recently, however, lawmakers perceived that this consensus had broken down, and they revised the tax code in response. This revision was once again undertaken ostensibly in the name of fairness. While the new code closed many loopholes in the former system, it also created a less progressive system by reducing the number of tax categories to two or three, and lowering the ceiling for tax rates. I do not wish to speculate here on the economic effects of these changes, but I would note that both the original tax code and its revision were advanced with the expressed purpose of making the system more fair, although the standards of fairness resulted in very different tax codes. Both systems also rely upon different notions of equity in assessing social costs.

Must we conclude that fairness has no meaning in these and other social decisions? I think not, but fairness is defined by reaching a public consensus about what constitutes a fair and equitable distribution of social costs. My previous considerations of time and the context of this problem apply again to the public opinion processes that underlie the creation of this consensus. Rawls justified his definition of fairness based upon the notion that individuals choose the rules for decision making from behind a "veil of ignorance" concerning others' interests and talents in the "original position" (i.e. before civil society is created). This "veil of ignorance" is a useful concept, but it is too static, as defined by Rawls, for my purposes here. The "veil of ignorance" is not just a construct that exists prior to the establishment of a society. We always make public choices from behind a veil of ignorance about others' opinions; we seek to pierce that veil if possible, to discover the dominant opinion in the society. The dominant opinion, in turn, defines a convention of equity or fairness for the time in which it holds sway.

Both Rawls and Barry are willing to accept that in the "original position," individuals are armed with "a body of psychological generalizations and some elements of social and economic theory. This enables them to predict (in certain respects) the implications of choosing one principle rather than another" (Barry, 1973:17). But we should not assume that this "body of generalizations" and the elements of social and economic theory are abandoned after the original position. Such an assumption would parallel, and define, the abandonment of "the public" once the state is created. Prior to each public choice, the "body of psychological generalizations" that individuals have at their disposal is the general fear of isolation. Similarly, the elements of social and economic theory relevant to these choices are derived through the person's "quasi-statistical sense" about the emerging opinion in a society. This information enables citizens, at each juncture in public decision making, to generate an appropriate definition of fairness. This publicly accepted definition, in turn, guides a fair distribution of social costs, and facilitates the general acceptance of public choices.

This argument raises two problems. First, it seems to imply that all definitions of fairness are arbitrary and based solely upon public perceptions that cannot be traced to any source. If this is the case, then how can fairness and equity be necessary elements, in any meaningful way, for the stability of democratic systems? Second, it calls into question our prior conclusion that a more or less equal distribution of social costs is the most efficient formula for insuring the success of collective action. The consensual process for reaching a definition of fairness could lead to gross inequalities in the distribution of social costs. It certainly need not lead to a more or less equal distribution, despite appeals for fairness. Why then, may social costs be successfully levied deferentially, even while their advocates claim they are levied fairly?

Of course, the majority may simply define fairness to suit its own purposes, and thereby claim a fair distribution of costs while it exploits the minority. But this explanation is unsatisfactory based upon my previous logic, for if individuals will reject a social decision approved by the majority if the costs to the contributors are too high, these individuals will also reject a definition of fairness that supposedly justifies those costs. The answer to the unequal distribution of social costs thus lies elsewhere.

I have assumed to this point in the model that the sensitivity to the fear of isolation is randomly distributed among groups in the society. Hence, exchange curves for C and C' should also be randomly distributed in any given space defined by these two values. However, we know this assumption to be incorrect. Certain social groups in a society tend to be more susceptible to the threat of isolation than other groups. Noelle-Neumann shows that while there is a general tendency for individuals not to express unpopular opinions, this tendency is stronger in certain subgroups in the population than in others. These subgroups often share characteristics that make them readily identifiable. She illustrates this point by testing the willingness of particular individuals to express the minority opinion regarding then Chancellor Brandt's performance in office in 1972. The minority opinion was more likely to be expressed publicly by men than women, young people than older people, more educated people than less educated people, and people in higher status occupations than people in lower status occupations (Noelle-Neumann, 1984:29). In each case, people in the latter group tended to be more sensitive to the threat of isolation than people in the former group. If these tendencies are generally known in the society, one would expect that social costs would tend to fall most heavily upon the groups made up of people who are most sensitive to isolation. These people would be the least likely to speak out when the majority prevailed upon them to bear a disproportionate share of the total cost of collective action, C_t. Indeed, this condition seems to occur in the United States: those who have more education and income and who require less from government are more likely to be heard than those who have less education and income and require more from government. In fact, this difference occurs even though the latter group sees government action as a solution to their problems, while the former group does not (see Verba and Nie, 1971:267–85).

Once again, the "latent groups" described at the end of the last chapter raise the second caveat to my discussion of fairness in the distribution of social costs for many who favor a more equitable distribution of social costs and benefits are members of the groups least likely to speak out. They are rendered latent or silent by the dominant definition of fairness that guides the assessment of social costs at any given time. These individuals are disadvantaged due to their stronger sensitivity to the threat of social isolation.

LIBERALISM, CONSERVATISM, AND INSTITUTIONAL ARRANGEMENTS

What, then, can be done about this problem in democratic societies, which depend upon the threat of isolation for stability? Clearly, my preliminary response to the second question raises doubts about stability and the equation of fairness and equity in such societies. Also, an axiomatic principle of fairness may not be imposed upon the population as a solution. This principle would be privileged and doctrinaire, and would thus necessarily conflict with the privileged and responsive democratic rule supported by the spiral of silence. But we need not reach the opposite conclusion that the principle of fairness needs to be abandoned in democratic societies (even supposing that these societies could exist under such conditions). Instead, the twin values of stability and fairness tend to be balanced in successful democratic societies by the application of liberal or conservative solutions to the problem of allocating social costs.

The liberal solution attempts to bring about a more equitable distribution of social costs in the society, even if these changes risk disrupting the present patterns of collective choice. This strategy usually involves building up an individual's group identification as a "barrier" of sorts to the threat of isolation from other members of the society. Organizers attempt to insulate group members from the threat of social isolation, in order to reach a more equal distribution of social costs, for as a group mobilizes, it requires a greater threat of isolation, C', to coerce its members to pay the same social costs. If there is no way for the majority to increase this threat, it must redistribute social costs to a point at which the minority is willing to once again exchange C for C'. The liberal solution assumes that given a generally acceptable degree of freedom, and a more or less equitable distribution of social costs, most or all citizens will be willing to pay C in exchange for C', so that collective choices may be made.

The conservative solution responds that the liberal strategy risks desensitizing group members to a point at which the threat of social isolation holds no sway over individuals' actions, for if mobilization may result in a more equitable distribution of costs, benefits, and rights, what will stop group members from demanding the lion's share of benefits and rights, while avoiding all social costs? If the threat of isolation may be reduced in the manner I have described, will it ever again be an effective device for coercing group members into exchanging costs to avoid social isolation? The result might simply be a disruption of social interactions or calls for separatism from the group's members. This conservative argument stresses the virtues of having a stable society, even if social costs are not always distributed equitably, since collective benefits for most members can still be created. This solution cautions whenever possible against reassessments of social costs, goods, and rights in a stable society. The goal of possible equity is subsumed under the reality that a balance does exist in which individuals will exchange values of C for C' in the stable society.

It is inappropriate to advocate either solution generally outside of the decision context in which it might be relevant. I would be remiss, though, if I did not attempt to describe, however vaguely, what a stable, fair, and equitable society would look like, and it would be unrealistic not to acknowledge that societies tend to rely upon institutions to provide a necessary degree of decision making stability. How do these observations fit into my discussion of the spiral of silence? The last few chapters have discussed the exchange values of C and C', and groups in society that are sensitive to the threat of isolation, as if these variables were in a constant state of flux. However, this is not the case in most stable democracies. Patterns and conventions develop over time to reflect the varying sensitivities individuals have to the threat of isolation and the relationships that form between them as a result. These individual relationships, patterns, and conventions (particularly of language) tend to be relatively stable over time. The study of these stable patterns, which are so critical to the processes of public opinion and public choice, is the study of institutions.

Recently, social choice theorists such as Ostrom (1986:3) and Riker (1980:20) have directed considerable attention toward institutions. Some observers explain the return to the study of institutions as a frustrated reaction to the unfulfilled promises of behavioralism. Some of the more recent approaches to the topic, however, raise several of the themes considered in this book.

Consider two recent attempts to define "institutions." Plott describes institutions as "rules for *individual expression, information transmittal,* and social choice" (Plott, 1979:156; emphases mine). In this definition, the author separates the process of social choice from the processes of preference expression and information transmittal. Schotter advances a similar idea; he notes that social institutions "are not rules of the game but rather the *alternative equilibrium standards of behavior or conventions of behavior that evolve from a given game described by its rules*. In other words, for us, *institutions are properties of the equilibrium of games and not properties of the game's description*. We care about what the agents do with the rules of the game, not what the rules are" (Schotter, 1981:155; emphases mine).

Plott's and Schotter's definitions, when combined, describe an equilibrium of "individual expression" and "information transmittal" existing outside of the formal rules governing social choice. Within Schotter's definition, for example, one may envision a system where all persons have the theoretical right to free expression, but where certain individuals are more likely to exercise this right than others. Neither author explicitly states whether the patterns of expression and communication precede the rules they describe, or grow out of those rules. Schotter seems to imply the latter, while Plott appears neutral on this score. However, if the patterns of expression and communication are separate from the formal rules, how did the formal rules come to exist? If these rules grew out of some form of tacit or stated agreement between individuals governed by those rules, then this agreement must have had to be communicated. We are back at the same point noted in chapter 2 when I stated Proposition I; we assume that the rules of expression and information transmittal that exist within institutions preceded the rules that govern those institutions. Public opinion precedes public choice, even in an institutional context.

Critics of this position may argue that the pattern of communication that must have preceded the establishment of institutional rules need not be the same pattern in the present institutional context. The rules created may have transformed the patterns of communication that existed prior to the origins of the institution, but this argument disregards the conventions of communication that allowed for the creation of rules in the first place. These conventions must be reflected in the decision-making institutions of responsive systems, or they will always be a potential threat to the rules governing those institutions. Also, to assume that one uses a means of expressing preferences in order to change the manner in which one expresses preferences runs afoul of a version of the Rule of Privileged Choice, for if some other rules for communication were preferable to the ones used to generate institutions, why were these rules not used to create the institutions in the first place?

If the institutional patterns of "expression and information transmittal" grow out of the public opinion process, then this process may explain the "institutional context" within which so many decisions take place. The context grows out of the varying sensitivities individuals have to the threat of social isolation. Assume that a clear pattern exists in a society, with groups less sensitive to isolation speaking out and groups more sensitive to isolation falling silent. Over time, an equilibrium emerges regarding who speaks and who is silent. Patterns of behavior for speech or silence become stable and somewhat predictable—*institutionalized*, if you will. A set of conventions of speech thus arises within which social choices are made.

All of this implies that the study of institutions, and the study of public opinion and behavior, are not as separate as social scientists have tended to make them, *for institutions arise out of patterns of speech or silencing that are stable over time, due to the varying group sensitivities to the threat of isolation*. Conversely, institutions may be disrupted when a social cost levied against a group is perceived as being "too high," or out of balance with that group's sensitivity to isolation. In Olson's terms, "latent" groups may become "privileged" groups when group members no longer accept the previous balance between C and C', due to a relative increase in the value of C. For this reason, liberals tend to have less reverence for institutions, being more willing to disrupt institutional arrangements in pressing for equitable distributions of social costs, than conservatives. Conservatives tend to argue that the conventions of speech or silence which arise from groups' differential sensitivities to isolation are proven useful—or even natural—by their role in guaranteeing social stability.

If institutions do reflect the underlying sensitivities individuals have to social isolation, what would be the ideal institutional arrangement? Such an arrangement would balance the demands of stability and fairness in some equilibrium that would require no more adjustment. All citizens would be sensitive enough to the threat of isolation to guarantee conformity to majority decisions reached through institutional means. Costs and benefits would be distributed equally or fairly enough that the fear of isolation would always be sufficient to enforce conformity. This arrangement would be necessary and sufficient to induce conformity to majority decisions. Certainly, it is this ideal of human interaction that gives fairness much of its moral and practical force as a decision making standard.

Given the variety of human possibilities, however, it is doubtful that any such necessary and sufficient arrangement exists, even for most members of society. It might prove technically impossible to prescribe a balance of C and C' for self-interested citizens assuming such a theoretical balance existed. Successful democratic societies are more likely to make do with piecemeal adjustments to the notion of fairness, and the distribution of social costs, through liberal and conservative solutions. The experimental or reverential attitudes toward institutions that the solutions respectively promote thus follow.

Barry and Hardin have argued that the Prisoners' dilemma problem is not a paradox, but a challenge to devise institutions to avoid it (Barry and Hardin, 1981:386). In this book, I have described a few means of avoiding the Prisoners' dilemma problem. One may adhere to a rule that is privileged and doctrinaire, or one may adhere to a rule that is privileged and responsive. Both solutions solve the problem, but entail very different strategies. If we are to rely upon institutional means in a responsive choice system to solve this problem, we would do best to be sensitive to the values of C and C', and the varying reactions groups have to the threat of isolation, in setting up the rules of those institutions. There need be no paradox, or condition where rules are contrary to received opinion, if we remain sensitive to the manner in which the spiral of silence variables manifest themselves in stable institutions.

CONCLUSION

It is appropriate that a discussion of the redefined notion of social preference conclude with a discussion of democratic institutions, for the creation of stable, responsive institutions constituted the third problem or paradox of public choice from the first chapter—that is, how any formula for social choice could define legitimate decision processes for a society. The answer lies in perceiving these processes, in an open or institutional context, as a reflection of the current state of public opinion in the society, with the patterns of expression and silencing among groups that this implies. By this means, democratic societies may create a public agenda (a version of the Arrow problem), generate public or collective goods (a version of the Olson problem), or create legitimate decision-making institutions. The redefined notion of social preference generates a convention of language in which one choice is set equivalent to the social preference, and the other choices are silenced. Conventions of language distinguish public concerns that must be discussed from private concerns that are left unexpressed; the result is a public agenda. Conventions of language distinguish public goals that demand support from private goals, which are the individual's own business; the result is the creation of public goods. Conventions of language distinguish the discourse of public institutions from the discourse of private conversations or thoughts; the results are patterns of expression or silencing that give certain groups advantages in the institutional context.

The notion of "public" inherent in the spiral of silence theorems runs as a theme through all of these solutions, for "public" is not defined explicitly by our individual preferences of what constitutes a public issue, public good, or public institution. Our sense of "public" in any decision grows out of our feeling of exposure to other individuals' preferences (and judgments) in the society. This feeling of exposure is an independent variable that determines the solidarity and stability of a society. Individual preferences may only become social preferences, or conventions of language about public things, when individuals share this feeling of exposure to their peers' judgments. The paradoxes of public choice are aptly named; they represent cases where individuals act contrary to received opinions, or the dominant opinion, concerning proper social behavior at a given time.

Ultimately, however, one must ask if such contrary behavior is always necessarily a bad thing. We are not, after all, so taken with the virtues of responsive choice systems that we argue majority opinions should always prevail in social decisions, even within the limits prescribed by a given set of values for C and C'. When the minority is in danger of being seriously harmed, the alternative of reaching no decision (as under a system of nonprivileged rules) becomes attractive. Similarly, there are surely cases in which the application of a doctrinaire rule is the best means of setting social policy. The analysis of the spiral of silence theorems should be taken as descriptive rather than prescriptive. Because responsive systems are a worthwhile goal in most cases, we should understand how the force of public opinion allows these systems to make public choices.

Our definition of "public" is thus represented in our most basic public activity, from which all other public acts allow—the creation of a common language for political and social discourse. It is for this reason that the rules governing the expression of opinions in the spiral of silence theory are so critical to the notion of "public choice." Paradoxes of public choice represent a society's failure to achieve a common public language: for what is contrary to common opinion is common silence.

NOTES

1. An example of this strategy can be seen in the design of automobiles. Each year, automobile manufacturers will make design changes in their cars, not necessarily to improve the automobiles, but rather so that individuals may distinguish one year's model from preceding or subsequent years' models. If an individual lives in a society that esteems new cars, then that individual must constantly be trading in his older model for a new one, simply because the older models are so easily distinguished from new ones. (The one exception to this rule, the Volkswagen Beetle, was discontinued when its potential market became prosperous enough to desire a car whose year might be easily distinguished for status reasons.)

2. Of course, there is nothing wrong with designing an axiomatic principle

that includes a specific time limit. The problem here, however, is that the time limit is *implicit*, and left unstated in the principle.

3. Indeed, it is interesting to note that many analysts will state their intention to discuss social decision making and then turn to institutional decision making to study the transitive rule. I would argue that once one discusses transitivity, one has already changed the decision making context from open to institutional.

4. Note that this situation could arise if the minority disagrees with the collective goal desired by the majority.

5. It is for this reason that I emphasized in chapter 5 how the spiral of silence theory advances the fear of isolation, not altruism or guilt, as a motivation for contributing to collective action.

Bibliography

Abrams, Robert. *Foundations of Political Analysis: An Introduction to the Theory of Collective Choice*. New York: Columbia University Press, 1980.

Ardener, Edwin. "Introductory Essay." In *Social Anthropology and Language*, edited by E. W. Ardener. London: Tavistock Press, 1971.

Ardener, Shirley. "Ground Rules and Social Maps for Women." In *Women and Space*, edited by Shirley Ardener. New York: St. Martin's Press, 1981.

Aristotle. *The Politics*. Translated and edited by Ernest Barker. New York: Oxford University Press, 1962.

Arrow, Kenneth J. *Social Choice and Individual Values*. New York: John Wiley and Sons, 1963.

———. "Current Developments in the Theory of Social Choice." *Social Research*, Vol. 4. In *Rational Man and Irrational Society?*, edited by Barry and Hardin, 1982.

———. "On the Agenda of Organization." In *The Economics of Information: Collected Papers of Kenneth Arrow, Vol. 4*. pp. 167–84. Cambridge: Harvard University, Belknap Press, 1984.

———. *Individual Choice Under Certainty and Uncertainty: Collected Papers of Kenneth Arrow, Vol. 3*. Cambridge: Harvard University, Belknap Press, 1984a.

Asch, Solomon. "Group Forces in the Modification and Distortion of Judgments." In *Social Psychology*, pp. 450–73. London: Routledge and Kegan Paul, 1952.

Axelrod, R. *The Evolution of Cooperation*. New York: Basic Books, 1984.

Barry, Brian. *Political Argument*. London: Routledge and Kegan Paul, 1965.

———. *The Liberal Theory of Justice: A Critical Examination of the Principal Doctrines in "A Theory of Justice" by John Rawls*. Oxford: Clarendon Press, 1973.

———. *Economists, Sociologists, and Democracy*. Chicago: University of Chicago Press, 1978.

——. "Is Democracy Special?" In *Philosophy, Politics, and Society, Fifth Series*. In *Rational Man and Irrational Society?*. Edited by Barry and Hardin, 1982.

Barry, Brian and Russell Hardin. *Rational Man and Irrational Society?* Beverly Hills: Sage Publications, 1982.

Bell, Daniel. "The Racket-Ridden Longshoremen: The Web of Economics and Politics." In *The End of Ideology: On the Exhaustion of Political Ideas in the Fifties*, pp. 175–209. New York: Free Press, 1960.

Black, Duncan. *The Theory of Committees and Elections*. Cambridge: Cambridge University Press, 1958.

Buchanan, James M. and Gordon Tullock. *The Calculus of Consent*. Ann Arbor: University of Michigan Press, 1962.

Campbell, Angus, Gerald Gurin and Warren E. Miller. *The Voter Decides*. Evanston, Ill.: Row, Peterson, and Co., 1954.

Childs, Harwood L. *Public Opinion: Nature, Formation, and Role*. Princeton: Von Nostrand, 1965.

Dahl, Robert and Charles E. Lindblom. *Politics, Economics, and Welfare*. New York: Harper and Row, 1953.

Downs, Anthony. *An Economic Theory of Democracy*. New York: Harper and Row, 1957.

Erikson, Robert S., Norman R. Luttberg and Kent L. Tedin. *American Public Opinion: Its Origins, Content, and Impact*. 3d ed. New York: Macmillan, 1988.

Fishburn, Peter C. "The Irrationality of Transitivity in Social Choice." *Behavioral Science*. 15 no.2 (1970):119–27.

Galbraith, John Kenneth. *The Affluent Society*. Boston: Houghton Mifflin, 1958.

Gibbard, Allan. "Manipulation of Voting Schemes." *Econometrica*. In *Rational Man and Irrational Society?* Edited by Barry and Hardin, 1982.

Glynn, Carroll J. and Jack M. McLeod. "Implications of the Spiral of Silence Theory for Communication and Public Opinion Research." In *Political Communication Yearbook*, edited by Dan Nimmo, Lynda Lee Kaid, and Keith Sanders. Carbondale: Southern Illinois Press, 1985.

Hadari, Savuiv. "A Review of *The Spiral of Silence*." *Ethics*. 96 (1985):213–14.

Hall, Edward T. *The Silent Language*. New York: Fawcett World Library, 1959.

Hardin, Russell. "Collective Action as an Agreeable n-Prisoners' Dilemma." *Behavioral Science*. 16 (1971):471–81.

——. *Collective Action*. Baltimore: Johns Hopkins Press for Resources for the Future, 1982.

Hirsch, Fred. *The Social Limits to Growth*. Cambridge: Harvard University Press, 1976.

Hofstadter, Douglas R. *Gödel, Escher, Bach: An Eternal Golden Braid*. New York: Random House, 1983.

Holicki, Sabine. *Isolationsdrohung—sozialpsychologische Aspekte einespublizistikwissenschaftlichen Konzepts*. Master's thesis, Institut für Publizistik, University of Mainz, 1984.

Hume, David. *Essays Moral, Political, and Literary*. London: Oxford University Press, 1963 [1741/1742].

Kepplinger, Hans Mathius. "Massenmedia: Macht ohne Verantwortung?" In

Reden Wir Morgen im Sprechblasen?, edited by Karl-Jugen Wilbert, pp. 70–83. Koblenz: Handweskammer, 1984.

Key, V. O. *Public Opinion and American Democracy*. New York: Alfred A. Knopf, 1961.

Ladd, Everett Carll. *Where Have All the Voters Gone?—The Fracturing of America's Political Parties*, 2d ed. New York: W. W. Norton and Co., 1982.

Lenin, V. I. *What Is To Be Done?*. New York: International Publications, 1929.

Lichtenstein, S. and P. Slovic. "Reversals of Preference Between Bids and Choices in Gambling Decisions." *Journal of Experimental Psychology*. 89 (1971):46–55.

Lindblom, Charles E. *Politics and Markets: The World's Political-Economic Systems*. New York: Basic Books, 1978.

Lipset, Seymour Martin and William Schneider. *The Confidence Gap: Business, Labor, and Government in the Public Mind*. New York: Free Press, 1983.

Little, I. M. D. "Social Choice and Individual Values." *Journal of Political Economy*. In *Rational Man and Irrational Society?*. Edited by Barry and Hardin, 1982.

Locke, John. *An Essay Concerning Human Understanding*. 2 Vols. Edited by Alexander Campbell Fraser. Oxford: Clarendon Press, 1894.

Mackie, J. L. "Fallacies." In *The Encyclopedia of Philosophy*. Vol. 3, pp. 169–79. New York: Macmillan. In Hardin, *Collective Action*, 1967.

Marx, Karl. "The Critique of the Gotha Program." In *Karl Marx and Frederick Engels: Selected Works*. New York: New World Paperbacks, 1972.

———. *Die Grundrisse*. London: Pelican Marx Library, 1973.

———. *Capital*, 3 Volumes. Edited by Frederick Engels. New York: International Publishers, 1975.

———. "Results of the Immediate Process of Production." In *Karl Marx: Selected Writings*, edited by David McLellan. Oxford: Oxford University Press, 1977.

Mason, Alpheus Thomas, William M. Beaney, and Donald Grier Stephenson, Jr. *American Constitutional Law: Introductory Essays and Selected Cases*. 7th ed. Englewood Cliffs, N.J.: Prentice-Hall, 1983.

May, Kevin D. "A Set of Independent Necessary and Sufficient Conditions for Simple Majority Decision." *Econometrica*. In *Rational Man and Irrational Society?*. Edited by Barry and Hardin, 1982.

Milgram, Stanley. "Nationality and Conformity." *Scientific American*. 105:45–51, 1961.

Mill, John Stuart. *On Liberty*. 1859. Reprint. New York: Bobbs-Merrill Co., 1956.

———. *A System of Logic*. London. In Barry, *Political Argument*, 1898.

National Opinion Research Center (N.O.R.C.). *General Social Surveys, 1972–1983: Cumulative Codebook*, edited by James A. Davis and Tom W. Smith. Storrs, Conn.: Roper Public Opinion Research Center, 1983.

Noelle-Neumann, Elisabeth. "Turbulences in the Climate of Opinion: Methodological Applications of the Spiral of Silence Theory." *Public Opinion Quarterly*. 41 (1977):143–58.

———. *Allensbacher Jahrbuch der Demoskopie, Band VII: 1976–1977*. Munich: Molden-Vevlag, 1977.

———. *Die Schweigespirale: Öffentliche Meinung—Unsere Soziale Haut*. Munich: R. Piper and Co., 1980.

——. *The Germans: Public Opinion Polls, 1967–1980*. Westport, Conn.: Greenwood Press, 1981.

——. "The Spiral of Silence: A Response." In *Political Communication Yearbook*, edited by Nimmo, et al., 1985.

——. *The Spiral of Silence: Public Opinion—Our Social Skin*. Chicago: University of Chicago Press, 1984.

——. "Identifying Opinion Leaders." *Proceedings of the 1985 ESOMER Conference*. pp. 173–200. Wiesbaden, 1985.

Olson, Mancur. *The Logic of Collective Action*. Cambridge: Harvard University Press, 1965.

Ostrom, Elinor. "An Agenda for the Study of Institutions." *Public Choice*. 48 (1986):3–25.

Plott, Charles R. "Axiomatic Social Choice Theory." *American Journal of Political Science*. In *Rational Man and Irrational Society?*. Edited by Barry and Hardin, 1982.

——. "The Application of Laboratory Experimental Methods to Public Choice." In *Collective Decision-Making: Applications from Public Choice Theory*, edited by C. S. Russell. Baltimore: Johns Hopkins University Press, 1979.

Prewitt, Kenneth and Sidney Verba. *An Introduction to American Government*, 4th ed. New York: Harper and Row, 1983.

Rae, Douglas W. "Decision Rules and Individual Values in Constitutional Choice." *American Political Science Review*. In *Rational Man and Irrational Society?*. Edited by Barry and Hardin, 1982.

Rappoport, Anatole. "Prisoners' Dilemma—Recollections and Observations." *Game Theory as a Theory of Conflict Resolution*. In *Rational Man and Irrational Society?*. Edited by Barry and Hardin, 1982.

Rawls, John. *A Theory of Justice*. Cambridge: Harvard University Press, 1971.

Riesman, David. *The Lonely Crowd*. New York: Anchor Books, 1950.

Riker, William. "Implications from the Disequilibrium of Majority Rule for the Study of Institutions." In *Political Equilibrium*. Edited by P. C. Ordeshook and K. A. Shepsle. Boston: Kluwer-Nijhoff. Originally published in the *American Political Science Review*. 74 (1980):432–47.

Riker, William and P. C. Ordeshook. "A Theory of the Calculus of Voting." *American Political Science Review*. 62 (1968):25–42.

Rusciano, Frank Louis. "Avoiding Arrow's Paradox in the Budget Process." *Proceedings of the 1984 American Political Science Association Convention*, 1984.

Sabia, Daniel R., Jr. "Rationality, Collective Action, and Karl Marx." *American Journal of Political Science*. 21 (1988):50–71.

Schelling, Thomas C. *Micromotives and Macrobehavior*. New York: W. W. Norton and Co., 1977.

Schotter, Andrew. *The Economic Theory of Institutions*. Cambridge: Cambridge University Press, 1981.

Scherif, H. "A Study of Social Factors in Perception." *Archives of Psychology*. 29 (1935):149.

——. *Psychology of Social Norms*. New York: Harper and Row, 1966.

Shubik, M. "Games Theory, Behavior and the Paradox of the Prisoners' Dilemma: Three Solutions." *Journal of Conflict Resolution*. 14 (1970):181–93.

Snidal, Duncan. "Coordination Versus Prisoners' Dilemma: Implications for International Cooperation and Regimes." *American Political Science Review*. 79 (1985):923–42.

Statistische Bundesamt. *Statistische Jahrbuch, 1967*. W. Kohlhammer: Mainz, 1986.

———. *Statistische Jahrbuch, 1985*. W. Kohlhammer: Mainz, 1985.

Taylor, D. Garth. "Pluralistic Ignorance and the Spiral of Silence: A Formal Analysis." *Public Opinion Quarterly*. 46 (1982):311–35.

Taylor, M. *Anarchy and Cooperation*. New York: Wiley and Sons, 1976.

Tönnies, Ferdinand. *Kritik der Öffentliche Meinung*. Berlin: Julius Springer, 1922.

Truman, David. *The Governmental Process*. New York: Alfred A. Knopf, 1952.

Tversky, Amos. "Intransitivity of Preferences." *Psychological Review*. 76 (1969):31–48.

Verba, Sidney and Norman H. Nie. *Participation in America*. New York: Harper and Row, 1972.

Yeric, Jerry L. and John R. Todd. *Public Opinions: The Visible Politics*. Itasca, N.Y.: F. E. Peacock, 1983.

Index

Abrams, Robert, 31
Ardener, Shirley, 20
Aristotle, 104
Arrow, Kenneth, 16, 17; defining "public choice," 4; dictatorship, 35; proof restated according to typology of decision rules, 41–42; reasonable conditions for decision-making, 36; *Social Choice and Individual Values*, 36, 62
Asch, Solomon, 18; relevance of experiment to collective action problem, 86

Barry, Brian: axiomatic bases for decision-making, 60; "contracting out" of labor contributions, 118; critique of Rawls, 115–16; democracy as a means of decision-making, 71; distributive questions, 66–67; fashion and "synthetic wants," 87; "formalism" in analysis of social choice, 20; "ideal-regarding" and "want-regarding" rules, 34, 40∠nguage, 16, 142; legitimate decision-making processes, 8; nationalism, 129; original choice of processes, 10; *Political Argument*, 16, 60, 142; tradeoffs between political principles, 101–102. *See also* Barry, Brian and Hardin, Russell
Barry, Brian and Hardin, Russell: defining social preference, 141–42; defining "paradox," 13, 74; expectations of rationality, 79; expression of preferences, 17; extra-rational motivations in collective action, 81, 136; inclination to accept responsive and transitive rules together, 73; individual and social transitivity, 61; institutional solutions to Prisoners' dilemma, 162; public television as collective good, 105; *Rational Man and Irrational Society?*, 59; rationality and transitivity, 145–46; variations on Prisoners' dilemma, 45; Voter's paradox, 59. *See also* Barry, Brian; Hardin, Russell
Bell, Daniel, 118
Black, Duncan, 61

About the Author

FRANK LOUIS RUSCIANO is Assistant Professor of Political Science at Rider College.